CANADA

ABDO
Publishing Company

CANADA

by Karen Latchana Kenney

Content Consultant
James W. Endersby, Director of Canadian Studies
University of Missouri

CREDITS

Published by ABDO Publishing Company, PO Box 398166, Minneapolis, MN 55439.
Copyright © 2013 by Abdo Consulting Group, Inc. International copyrights reserved
in all countries. No part of this book may be reproduced in any form without written
permission from the publisher. The Essential Library™ is a trademark and logo of
ABDO Publishing Company.

Printed in the United States of America,
North Mankato, Minnesota
112012
012013

♻ THIS BOOK CONTAINS AT LEAST 10% RECYCLED MATERIALS.

Editor: Lisa Owings
Series Designer: Emily Love

About the Author: Karen Latchana Kenney is a freelance author and editor from
Minneapolis, Minnesota. She has written more than 70 educational books, including
Countries of the World: Iran. Her books have received positive reviews in Booklist,
Library Media Connection, and School Library Journal. Kenney loves to travel and has
visited Canada, Guyana, Ireland, and many other countries in Europe.

Cataloging-in-Publication Data

Kenney, Karen Latchana.
 Canada / Karen Latchana Kenney.
   p. cm. -- (Countries of the world)
Includes bibliographical references and index.
ISBN 978-1-61783-627-5
1. Canada--Juvenile literature.   I. Title.
971--dc22

                                   2012946076

Cover: Moraine Lake in Banff National Park, Alberta, Canada

TABLE OF CONTENTS

CHAPTER 1
A VISIT TO CANADA

After a long drive north from the eastern United States, you step out of your car into what seems like old Europe. With the city's narrow cobblestone streets and quaint buildings, it is hard to tell the difference. But you've really arrived in Old Quebec City in the province of Quebec, Canada. French explorers founded this fortified city as New France more than 400 years ago. And throughout the centuries, it has kept its distinctly French culture and ambience.

The city is split in two: Haute-Ville (Upper Town) and Basse-Ville (Lower Town). You first make your way up Cap Diamant (Cape Diamond) to the Upper Town. You see a structure that dominates the view from the top—Château Frontenac. It looks like a fairy-tale castle, but it was really built as a stopover hotel for railway travelers in 1893. A guided tour of the hotel is next, and you peek out of its windows to see an amazing view of the

Château Frontenac holds the Guinness World Record for being the most photographed hotel in the world.

Château Frontenac towers above the beautiful city of Quebec, Canada.

QUEBEC'S ICE HOTEL

For a unique stay in Quebec, book a room at the Hôtel de Glace, or "Ice Hotel." Made completely of ice, it is open from the first week in January to the last week in March. Inside its thick walls, the temperature hovers between 23 and 27 degrees Fahrenheit (-5 and -3°C). Guests sleep inside special Arctic sleeping bags on beds set in solid ice frames. Each year, the hotel is completely remodeled. It is filled with ice sculptures and beautifully carved rooms with a new theme each year. The 2012 theme was "The Northern Quebec," and the hotel's design focused on the art, culture, knowledge, and values of the native peoples of Canada.

city and the Saint Lawrence River winding below.

To truly see the sights, you take a walk on the fortified wall of the Upper Town, the only walled city in North America. Built between the seventeenth and nineteenth centuries, the wall spans 2.9 miles (4.6 km) and was Quebec's defense system for centuries.[1] Today, the restored walls provide spectacular views of the river and city below.

After all that walking, you've worked up a thirst and an appetite. You settle down at a sidewalk café and enjoy a steaming bowl of café au lait to combat the chill in the air. To satisfy your hunger, you try a real French-Canadian dish—poutine. This decadent dish is made from crispy French fries covered with brown gravy and cheese curds. It was created

The Hôtel de Glace, or "Ice Hotel," in Quebec, Canada

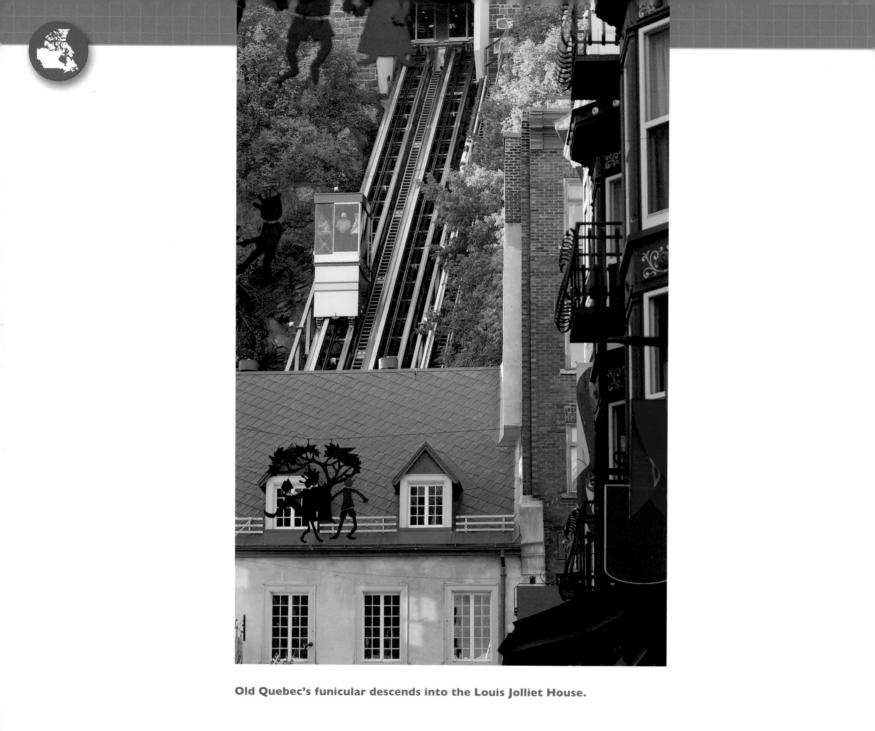

Old Quebec's funicular descends into the Louis Jolliet House.

in Quebec and has since spread throughout Canada.

Once you've recharged, it's time to explore the Lower Town. For a quick and easy route down, you take the funicular. This mountainside railroad was first built in 1879 and most recently remodeled in 1998. You enter at the Dufferin Terrace just outside the Château Frontenac. From your seat in the funicular car's glass cabin, you watch the scenery as you descend into the Lower Town. At the bottom, you exit into the historic Louis Jolliet House near Place Royale.

"How do les Québécois do winter so beautifully? It's a heady, head-clearing, steely-blue cold they summon here, but suffused with a supreme sense of warmth. Everyone absorbs a piece of the cold, so you don't have to do it alone."[2]

—*Annie Graves, travel writer*

You are excited to see Place Royale. It has existed for more than 400 years and was the first settled area of Quebec City. Seventeenth- and eighteenth-century buildings still surround this plaza, including the oldest stone church in North America—Notre-Dame des Victoires, or "Our Lady of Victories." At the center of the plaza is a bust of King Louis XIV, which was originally erected in 1686.

To end your day, you stroll through the Quartier Petit Champlain. This area is filled with boutiques and bistros. You look up to see the beautiful trompe-l'oeil mural—a painting that creates an optical illusion—

on a building owned by artisans of the area. It depicts the origins of the neighborhood and the trials its residents have endured throughout the centuries. What are you looking to buy? You find arts and crafts, jewelry, clothing, and plenty of pastries and sweets. But most of all, it is just a beautiful area, perfect for wandering aimlessly. With all the sites you've seen and experiences you've had in one day, you understand why Old Quebec City is such a valued historical treasure in Canada and around the world.

DIVERSE LAND, DIVERSE PEOPLE

Old Quebec City is just a small portion of the immense country Canada has become. The country is the second largest in the world, with geography ranging from Arctic tundra to grassy plains and from mountains to rain forest.[3] Within that diverse landscape lives a diverse people. Not only can you find French and British culture, but there are also native peoples, new immigrant communities, and descendants of

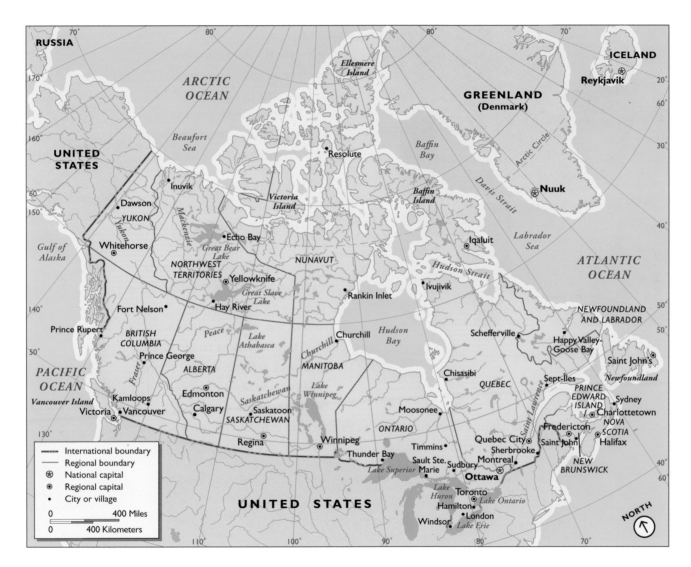

Political Boundaries of Canada

People in Toronto, Canada, celebrate their
nation's tolerance and diversity.

immigrants. Canadians prefer to think of their country not as a melting pot but rather as a mosaic of cultures, promoting diversity instead of one unified Canadian culture.

Despite the fact that Canada shares a long border with the United States and most of its people live near that border, Canadians strongly maintain a separate identity. They know they are not Americans, but it is sometimes hard for Canadians to identify who they are as a whole. Many believe diversity, tolerance, and nonviolence are the defining characteristics of Canadian culture. Within that culture, the many different peoples of Canada continue to define what being Canadian means to them.

SNAPSHOT

Official name: Canada

Capital city: Ottawa

Form of government: a parliamentary democracy, a federation, and a constitutional monarchy

Title of leaders: prime minister (head of government); king or queen of the United Kingdom represented by Canada's governor-general (head of state)

Currency: Canadian dollar

Population (July 2012 est.): 34,300,083
World rank: 35

Size: 3,855,103 square miles (9,984,670 sq km)
World rank: 2

Languages: English and French

Official religion: none

Per capita GDP (2011, US dollars): $41,100
World rank: 20

CHAPTER 2

GEOGRAPHY: AN ANCIENT AND WILD LAND

In the vast expanse of Canada, you can find practically any geographic feature. Mountain ranges grace both the east and west coasts. Ocean coastlines, long rivers, and numerous lakes occupy the land. Prairies, lowlands, and rain forest are found here too. But Canada's largest geologic feature is the rocky Canadian Shield. This huge formation covers 3 million square miles (8 million sq km), approximately half of Canada's total area.[1] It wraps around the great Hudson Bay, stretching from the Atlantic Ocean to the Great Lakes and up to the Arctic Ocean. It spans across six provinces and two territories in Canada. Small parts of the shield extend into the US states of Michigan, Minnesota, New York, and Wisconsin.

Flowerpot Island in Ontario's Georgian Bay displays the rugged beauty of the Canadian Shield.

VOLCANOES IN CANADA

Some of the oldest volcanoes in the country are on the Canadian Shield. They are all silent today, with the last eruptions occurring more than 100 years ago, but many have the potential to erupt in the future. The most recent eruption was at Lava Fork in northwestern British Columbia approximately 150 years ago.

The Canadian Shield is made from Precambrian rock, which is more than 570 million years old. The shield lies where ancient mountain ranges once rose, though these mountain ranges no longer exist. During the Pleistocene epoch 2.6 million to 11,700 years ago, massive continental glaciers scraped the shield smooth as they moved south across the land. Today, the mountain ranges are rounded, rocky hills that reach an average height of 100 feet (30 m).[2] The shield has many shallow lake basins and a thin layer of soil. Boreal forests of spruce, fir, tamarack, and pine trees grow from this soil. These sprawling evergreen forests are ideal for hunting and trapping and are rich with raw minerals. The ancient Canadian Shield is an awe-inspiring example of the raw, rugged beauty that exists in the many wild areas of Canada.

BORDERS, PROVINCES, AND TERRITORIES

Canada has a total area of 3,855,103 square miles (9,984,670 sq km).[3] It is second in size only to Russia. The country sits atop North America and shares a land border with only one other country—the United States. Surrounding the rest of Canada are three oceans: the Pacific in the west, the Atlantic in the east, and the Arctic in the north.

Along the west coast is the province of British Columbia. The major metropolis Vancouver is in British Columbia, but the province's capital is Victoria on Vancouver Island. The many other islands off the coast include the Haida Gwaii archipelago. Above British Columbia is the Yukon Territory, which borders Alaska. The territories of the Yukon, the Northwest Territories, and Nunavut make up northern Canada.

In central and southern Canada are the provinces of Alberta, Saskatchewan, Manitoba, and Ontario. Alberta is well known for its cities of Calgary and Edmonton. Canada's largest

HAIDA GWAII

The Canadian islands of Haida Gwaii, or "Islands of the People," lie off the mainland of British Columbia. Approximately 150 islands fill this area, boasting mountains, forest plains, plateaus, and muskeg bogs. Three fault lines run through the islands. These have produced the strongest earthquake in Canada's history—an 8.1-magnitude quake that hit in 1949.

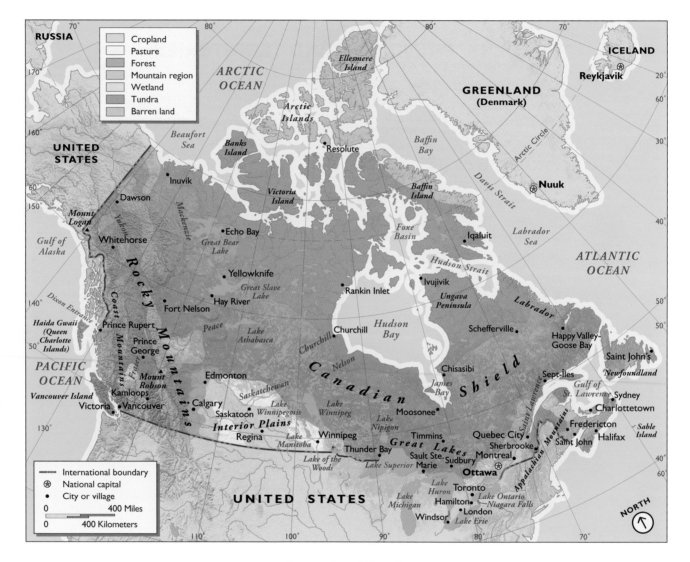

Geography of Canada

city, Toronto, is also the capital of Ontario. The nation's capital, Ottawa, is in eastern Ontario on the border with Quebec.

The provinces of Quebec, Nova Scotia, Prince Edward Island, New Brunswick, and Newfoundland and Labrador make up eastern Canada. Quebec City is the capital of Quebec. Canada's second-largest city, Montreal, is another important city in the province.

THE ARCTIC AND TAIGA LANDS

Canada and its provinces occupy six distinct geographic regions. The Arctic and taiga lands of northern Canada are vast, covering 1 million square miles (2.6 million sq km).[4] The Arctic is mostly a treeless frozen tundra with only low-growing vegetation. Farther south in the taiga region, some areas have forests of thin spruce and fir trees, along with large

THE ARCTIC TUNDRA

The tundra is the coldest biome on Earth. Minimal vegetation, poor nutrients, and little snow or rainfall characterize this biome. The tundra circles the North Pole and extends down to the coniferous forests of the taiga. Summers in the tundra last between 50 and 60 days. During this short growing season, lichens, mosses, low shrubs, sedges, and many kinds of flowers grow. The sun stays above the horizon 24 hours a day for some periods of the summer. In winter, there may be no daylight at all for many days.

wetlands. Within the Arctic and taiga regions are ice-covered mountains, fjords, ice floes, waterfalls, and stark river valleys. Northern Canada also includes many islands, such as Banks, Victoria, and Baffin Islands. The uplands of Ellesmere Island boast many mountains. The highest peak on this island is Barbeau Peak, which reaches 8,583 feet (2,616 m).[5] The largest river in Canada also flows through the north—the Mackenzie River. The entire river system is 2,635 miles (4,241 km) long.[6]

The far north is frozen year-round. In the other areas of the Arctic region, it is winter for most of the year. In the middle of winter, some parts of northern Canada receive no daylight at all. Canadian winters are bitterly cold. Summers are short and cool, lasting one to four months, but the days can be very long.

THE ROCKIES AND CORDILLERA

In the far west of Canada is the mountainous region of the Cordillera. This is where the Rockies continue from the United States into Canada. The Coast Mountains start near Vancouver and continue north as well. The highest peak in Canada is found here. Mount Logan reaches 19,551 feet (5,959 m).[7] The Cordillera occupies approximately 16 percent of Canada, or 620,000 square miles

Mount Logan is the second-highest peak in North America, after Alaska's Mount McKinley.

Bright spots around the sun, often called sun dogs, occur in Canada's Northwest Territories. They appear when ice crystals in the air reflect light from the sun.

The Canadian Rockies are dotted with scenic lakes.

(1.6 million sq km).[8] Along with rugged mountains, this area includes plateaus, valleys, and plains. The Cordillera also has several volcanoes, which have erupted sporadically over the centuries. And along the southern edge of the region grows a temperate rain forest.

The Cordillera stretches far north. One side faces the Pacific Ocean, and the other side faces Canada's interior. This makes for a wide variety of climates in the area. Rain and snow fall frequently on the Coast Mountains. Glaciers and snowfields are found at lower elevations. Mild, wet weather can be found along the coast. Summers are warm with some rain, and winters are colder and wetter. The interior areas are

AVERAGE TEMPERATURE AND PRECIPITATION

Region (City)	Average January Temperature Minimum/Maximum	Average July Temperature Minimum/Maximum	Average Precipitation January/July
Alberta (Edmonton)	-2.4/17.6°F (-19.1/-8°C)	49.1/72°F (9.5/22.2°C)	0.9/3.8 inches (2.3/9.7 cm)
British Columbia (Vancouver)	32.9/43°F (0.5/6.1°C)	55.8/71.1°F (13.2/21.7°C)	5.7/1.2 inches (14.5/3 cm)
Northwest Territories (Yellowknife)	-8.9/23.6°F (-22.7/-4.7°C)	54.3/70°F (12.4/21.1°C)	0.5/1.4 inches (1.3/3.6 cm)
Nunavut (Iqaluit)	-8.5/23.1°F (-22.5/-4.9°C)	38.7/52.9°F (3.7/11.6°C)	0.9/2.2 inches (2.3/5.6 cm)
Prince Edward Island (Charlottetown)	10/26°F (-12.2/-3.3°C)	58/73°F (14.4/22.8°C)	3.8/3 inches (9.7/7.6 cm)
Quebec (Montreal)	7/21°F (-13.9/-6.1°C)	56/73°F (13.3/22.8°C)	2.8/3.4 inches (7.1/8.6 cm)
Yukon (Whitehorse)	-8.9/6.6°F (-22.7/-14.1°C)	46.8/70.3°F (8.2/21.3°C)	0.7/1.7 inches (1.8/4.3 cm)[9]

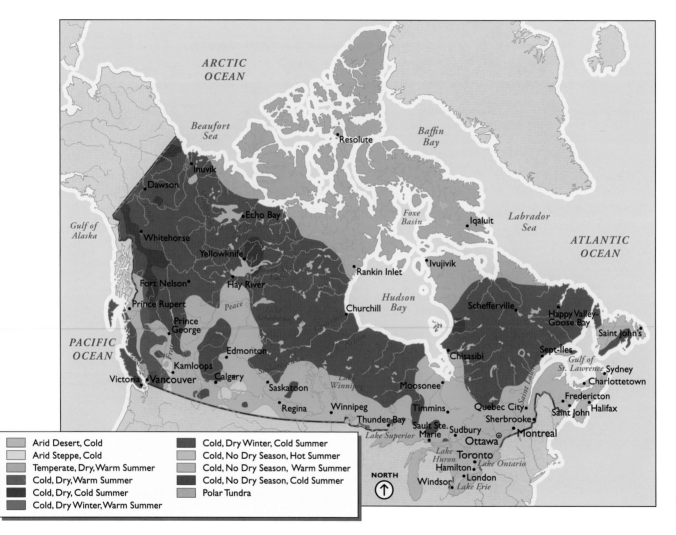

ARCTIC OCEAN

Beaufort Sea

• Resolute

Baffin Bay

• Inuvik

• Dawson

• Echo Bay

Foxe Basin

Labrador Sea

Gulf of Alaska

• Iqaluit

ATLANTIC OCEAN

• Whitehorse

• Yellowknife

• Ivujivik

• Rankin Inlet

• Fort Nelson

• Hay River

Peace

Hudson Bay

• Schefferville

• Happy Valley-Goose Bay

• Prince Rupert

• Churchill

• Saint John's

• Prince George

PACIFIC OCEAN

• Edmonton

• Chisasibi

Gulf of St. Lawrence

• Sept-Iles

• Sydney

• Kamloops

• Calgary

• Saskatoon

Lake Winnipeg

• Moosonee

• Charlottetown

• Victoria • Vancouver

• Fredericton

• Halifax

• Regina

• Winnipeg

• Timmins

• Quebec City

• Saint John

• Thunder Bay

• Sherbrooke

Lake Superior

• Sault Ste. Marie

• Sudbury

• Montreal

• Ottawa

Lake Huron

• Toronto

Lake Ontario

• Hamilton

NORTH
↑

• Windsor

• London

Lake Erie

Arid Desert, Cold	Cold, Dry Winter, Cold Summer
Arid Steppe, Cold	Cold, No Dry Season, Hot Summer
Temperate, Dry, Warm Summer	Cold, No Dry Season, Warm Summer
Cold, Dry, Warm Summer	Cold, No Dry Season, Cold Summer
Cold, Dry, Cold Summer	Polar Tundra
Cold, Dry Winter, Warm Summer	

Climate of Canada

dry and very warm in the summer while being very cold in the winter. Temperatures vary by altitude in the Cordillera. In the mountains, average temperatures rarely go above 50 degrees Fahrenheit (10°C). East of the mountains and in the country's interior, the weather is much warmer.

INTERIOR PLAINS

To the east of the Rockies and toward the middle of Canada are the Interior Plains. This area is made up of two ecozones: the Prairies and the Boreal Plains. The Prairies cover a low-lying area of valleys and plains, with the United States border to the south. The Prairies are mostly used for farming. This area is sometimes called the "Breadbasket of Canada." The mountains to the west block the humid air from the coast, so this area can become arid. Winters here are long and cold, though the short summers are relatively warm.

On the northern edge of the Prairies lie the Boreal Plains. Boreal forests cover much of this wild area. Like the Prairies, the land is filled with valleys and plains. Freshwater is abundant, with the largest body of water being Lake Winnipeg. The Boreal Plains get more precipitation than the Prairies do. Winters can be very cold, and summers are short and mild.

It is thought there are approximately 2 million lakes in Canada.

MIXEDWOOD PLAINS AND THE GREAT LAKES

Along the northern edges of the Great Lakes and including the Saint Lawrence River Valley are the Mixedwood Plains. The land is flat, rich, and fertile. Some of the region's features include the Oak Ridges Moraine, the Niagara Escarpment, and the Niagara Peninsula. The Oak Ridges Moraine contains the headwaters for 65 river systems, and wetlands, woodlands, streams, kettle bogs, and kettle lakes are abundant in the area. The Niagara Escarpment supports rare plants and animals in its wetlands and large wooded areas. The incredible Niagara Falls cascade from the Niagara Peninsula. Also in the Mixedwood Plains is the southernmost point of Canada's mainland—Point Pelee. It is an 11-mile- (18 km) long peninsula that extends into Lake Erie.[10] Winters are mild in this area because it is surrounded by water, and summers are pleasantly warm.

NIAGARA FALLS

Niagara Falls is truly a beautiful sight to behold. Its sheer size, its deafening roar, and the clouds of mist at its base make the falls majestic and ethereal. The falls are part of the Niagara River, which marks the border between Canada and the United States. Niagara Falls has three sets of waterfalls. On the US side are the Bridal Veil Falls and American Falls. On the Canadian side are the larger Horseshoe Falls. The Horseshoe Falls are 2,200 feet (670 m) wide and drop 188 feet (57 m).[11]

THE ATLANTIC REGION

Along the eastern edge of Canada is the Atlantic region. It has the Appalachian Mountains, 7,000 miles (11,200 km) of shoreline on the Atlantic Ocean, forested uplands, and fertile lowlands.[12] The highest peak in this area is Mount Carleton, which reaches 2,648 feet (807 m).[13] This area also has many lakes, streams, and rivers. Off the coast are almost 4,000 islands, many with lagoons and marshes.[14] Long, mild winters are typical of this area, and summers are cool.

Canada's magnificent Niagara Falls

CHAPTER 3

ANIMALS AND NATURE: ABUNDANT LIFE IN CANADA'S BIOMES

Fur, particularly beaver fur, made Canada the country it is today. It is incredible that a rodent would leave such a big mark on Canadian history. European fashion increased the demand for beaver fur in the seventeenth and eighteenth centuries. When explorers discovered the millions of beavers that inhabited Canada, the country became a fur-trading capital. Because of this link between fashion and fate, the beaver has become a national emblem of Canada's rich heritage, appearing on coins, crests, and newspaper mastheads.

Beavers are the largest rodents in North America and the second-largest rodents in the world. Only the capybara of South America is bigger. Beavers live throughout North America in ponds, marshes,

The beaver is Canada's national animal.

rivers, and wetlands. These amazing engineers cut down trees with their teeth and drag them into the water to form dams and lodges. They live in the lodges with their families. Their dams also help other species survive. Dams disrupt the water flow, increasing the water pooled in and around a river or stream. Some animals that benefit from this are brook trout, aquatic birds, river otters, and moose.

Beavers can be found throughout Canada up to the tundra. Although today their populations are growing, beavers were once close to extinction in Canada. After 200 years of uncontrolled trapping, beavers were exterminated in some areas. Today, licenses and limited trapping seasons control the number of beavers killed in Canada. Beavers are now thriving throughout the country.

Although beavers are an integral part of Canada's history, they are only one of many species in the country. With its many biomes, Canada is home to a diverse animal and plant population.

ARCTIC AND TAIGA SURVIVORS

Despite the harsh landscape and climate, polar bears, musk oxen, caribou, grizzly bears, lemmings, Arctic hares, and the Arctic fox thrive on Canada's frozen tundra. Seals, walrus, Arctic char, and whales—including belugas and narwhals—live in the sea. Some birds in the

Beluga whales swim off Canada's Arctic coasts.

tundra include the eider duck, Arctic terns, and jaegers. The ground is permanently frozen in the tundra, so no trees can grow. Only plants with shallow root systems thrive in the Arctic's brief summers. These plants include shrubs, grasses, fungi, lichens, and mosses. Many flowers grow too, including forget-me-nots, Arctic poppies, and saxifrage.

> The boreal forests were named after Boreas, the Greek god of the north wind.

Moving south into the taiga, the numbers and types of species increase. Woodland and forest-tundra give way to boreal forests, which stretch across northern Canada and into Alaska. The boreal forest is Canada's largest biome, characterized by its abundance of coniferous trees.[1] These include spruce, fir, tamarack, and pine. Many broad-leaved trees also grow there, such as birch, poplar, willow, alder, and mountain ash. Large carnivores in this ecosystem include bears, wolves, and lynx. Woodland caribou graze on vegetation that takes 100 years to grow. Moose, the largest members of the deer family, roam the forest eating aquatic plants and parts of deciduous trees. Many kinds of waterfowl live in the forest too, including the American black duck, mallard, blue-winged teal, and northern shoveler. Land birds include the warbler.

DIVERSITY OF THE CORDILLERA

Many types of trees grow in the varied landscapes of the Cordillera, such as the Rocky Mountain ponderosa pine, the Rocky Mountain red cedar, and the balsam poplar. In the temperate rain forest, rare orchids and ferns can be found.

Large herbivores such as caribou, deer, elk, bighorn sheep, moose, and mountain goats live in the Cordillera. In addition to black and grizzly bears, other large carnivores include the wolf, lynx, bobcat, and cougar. Smaller animals include the yellowbelly marmot, beaver, red fox, wolverine, mink, and striped skunk.

Owls, hawks, turkey vultures, and other birds of prey fly over the Cordillera. There are also shore and seabirds, including the black tern and the sandpiper. Songbirds include the black-billed magpie and purple finch. Some kinds of waterfowl are the sandhill crane and the Canada goose. Birds of the forest include the blue grouse and the chukar.

Sockeye salmon and sturgeon come to the Cordillera to spawn. The wood frog and long-toed salamander are there too. Snakes include the rubber boa and the western rattlesnake. And the red turpentine beetle and migratory grasshopper are just two of the many insects found in the Cordillera.

PRAIRIE AND PLAINS DWELLERS

The trees of Canada's prairie lands include the wolf willow, chokecherry, and balsam poplar. Other vegetation includes sagebrush, yellow cactus, and cattail. The black bear is the only large carnivore. Coyotes,

More than 500 species of Canadian plants and animals are considered to be at risk.

BISON

Millions of bison used to roam Canada's prairies until they were hunted almost to extinction. Now, small herds roam in protected areas of British Columbia, Saskatchewan, and the Northwest Territories. In Canada, there are at least 1,000 wild or semi-wild bison.[2] This species is considered to be threatened.

river otters, and striped skunks are some of the smaller carnivores. Rodents include the beaver, black-tailed prairie dog, and northern pocket gopher. The burrowing owl, ruby-throated hummingbird, and whooping crane are just a few of the many prairie birds. Many insects are also found there, including the monarch butterfly and pallid-winged grasshopper.

Elk, caribou, deer, moose, and bighorn sheep graze on the Boreal and Mixedwood Plains. Large hunters there include bears, wolves, bobcats, and lynx. Smaller animals found on the plains are the wolverine, fox, bat, and snowshoe hare. Walleye, sturgeon, trout, and whitefish swim in the rivers and lakes. Some birds include the loon, red-tailed hawk, and great blue heron. Trees and plants that grow well on the plains include the maple tree that is a national emblem for Canada.

Bison graze on Canada's prairie lands.

THE BOREAL AND ATLANTIC

The millions of lakes and rivers in the Boreal Shield make perfect habitats for amphibians, fish, and mollusks. Walleye, largemouth bass, and trout are abundant. Salamanders, frogs, and the redbelly snake also live here. The many kinds of birds include the Atlantic puffin and herring gull. Immense bowhead and blue whales share the seas with humpback whales, orcas, and seals. Atlantic salmon swim into Canadian rivers and streams to spawn. And the large muskellunge swim in the freshwater lakes of the area. Mammals in this region include porcupines, raccoons, and coyotes. The Boreal Shield has both coniferous and deciduous trees, and blueberries, water lilies, and shield ferns grow well too.

BOWHEAD WHALES

The gigantic bowhead whale eats the smallest creatures on Earth—plankton. It lives in the Arctic waters around Canada and has a 17- to 19-inch (43 to 50 cm) layer of blubber to protect it from the cold. These elusive whales are believed to be some of the longest-living mammals on Earth. Their lifespan may be between 100 and 200 years. To protect these whales, Canada created the first bowhead whale sanctuary in the world, the Ninginganiq National Wildlife Area.

The leaves on many Canadian maple trees turn red in autumn. A red maple leaf appears on the country's flag.

Along the southern Atlantic coast is the Atlantic maritime ecosystem. This area contains younger forests of spruce, birch, and maple. Many flowers, such as violets, lady's slippers, and starflowers also grow here. The few large carnivores include bears and bobcats. Smaller animals, such as the northern flying squirrel, muskrat, and woodchuck, are more common. In the ocean swim seals, the northern bottlenose whale, and the mighty blue whale. Many kinds of crustaceans are found there as well, including lobsters, crabs, and shrimps. Sea turtles also live in the ocean waters. Loggerheads, leatherbacks, and the Atlantic ridley are found there. And many songbirds, waterfowl, and birds of prey fly the skies above this coastal land.

SABLE ISLAND HORSES

Herds of wild horses live on the rugged Sable Island off the shore of Nova Scotia, home to a future national park. The horses are believed to be the descendants of 60 horses shipped there by a merchant in 1760. They live in small herds with several mares and one stallion. Their fur gets thick and shaggy in winter to protect them from the cold. There are thought to be approximately 300 to 400 wild horses living there today.[3]

NATIONAL PARKS

The world's first national park system was created in 1911 to protect and preserve the many wild places in Canada. Some of Canada's 44 national parks and park reserves are known for their historical value, such as Gwaii Haanas on Haida Gwaii, which preserves

First Nations' villages, totem poles, and archaeological sites.[4] Other parks are known for their isolated wilderness, such as Quttinirpaaq, the world's northernmost park. Some Canadian parks are especially good for seeing wildlife, such as Wapusk in Manitoba, where polar bears live in the wild. Several of Canada's parks are so precious they have been designated as UNESCO World Heritage Sites. They include Kluane along the border with Alaska in the north, Nahanni in the Northwest Territories, Gros Morne on the Newfoundland coast, Banff in Alberta, and Yoho in British Columbia.

The totem poles of Gwaii Haanas

ENVIRONMENTAL THREATS

Pollution due to human waste and industrial activities is a major threat to Canada's air, water, and soil. Air pollution causes acid rain that damages the soil, water, and plants. Mercury in the air can be deposited through rainfall, damaging wildlife habitat and food quality. Toxic rain is especially damaging to aquatic ecosystems.

ENDANGERED SPECIES IN CANADA

According to the International Union for Conservation of Nature (IUCN), Canada is home to the following numbers of species that are categorized by the organization as Critically Endangered, Endangered, or Vulnerable:

Mammals	12
Birds	15
Reptiles	5
Amphibians	1
Fishes	35
Mollusks	3
Other Invertebrates	10
Plants	2
Total	83[6]

Climate change is another big threat, especially in Canada's Arctic regions. Since 1948, Canada's overall climate has risen by 2.3 degrees Fahrenheit (1.3°C).[5] The country's Arctic areas have less snow cover, sea ice, and permafrost, and glaciers and ice caps have retreated. Glaciers are disappearing in the south, and snow is melting earlier. The icy habitat needed by many Canadian animals is shrinking. In response to climate change, some animals are migrating north, upsetting the natural balance even more. Climate change has also decreased the water levels in Canada's ponds and lakes. These changes could result in the extinction or forced

Climate change is causing ice caps in the Canadian Arctic to shrink, threatening polar bears and other Arctic animals.

adaptation of many Canadian animals and plants. In response, Canada's government has taken aggressive steps toward reducing the emissions of greenhouse gases within Canada and around the world.

Loss of habitat and wildlife is also of concern in Canada. This can be caused by environmental contamination, climate change, overharvesting, or the presence of invasive species. These changes threaten the health of an ecosystem and may have long-term negative effects.

CHAPTER 4

HISTORY: FROM FRONTIER TO INDEPENDENCE

Long before European explorers set foot on Canadian land, ancient peoples developed thriving communities there. Evidence found on Haida Gwaii suggests humans inhabited the islands up to 12,000 years ago. One of the largest sites of ancient human occupation in Canada is Debert in central Nova Scotia, where remains date to 11,000 years ago. Grant Lake, west of Hudson Bay, was first occupied approximately 8,000 years ago. And the northern Arctic area of Kettle Lake shows signs of humans from approximately 4,500 years ago.

The name Canada comes from the aboriginal word *kanata*, or "settlement."

The First Nations peoples were Canada's earliest inhabitants.

FIRST NATIONS

Early inhabitants had to be resourceful to survive Canada's harsh climate. Now known as the First Nations, the aboriginal peoples formed tribal groups, or bands, throughout Canada. They crossed the rough terrain using canoes, snowshoes, and dogsleds. Each band developed different lifestyles according to the resources available in their region.

The Algonquin and Athabascan peoples of the northern forest were skilled hunters who used every part of the animals they killed. They were constantly moving from one hunting ground to the next. In contrast, the Iroquoian peoples farmed along the eastern parts of Canada, around the Saint Lawrence River and in southern Ontario. These native bands lived in highly organized settlements with thousands of residents. Permanent longhouses served as their homes, which differed greatly from the temporary conical structures of the hunters. The Iroquoians developed farming techniques and grew corn, beans, squash, and sunflowers. The hunters and the Iroquoians regularly traded with each other and established trading routes long before Europeans arrived.

The Canadian government adopted the term *First Nations* after aboriginal Canadians began using it.

The plains peoples survived mainly on bison and developed effective hunting methods for the large animals. They also hunted red deer and smaller animals and were adept at fishing. They moved from summer villages to winter camps throughout the year. The tribes of the west coast were great at fishing and trading. Salmon was the prized catch for both food and trade. These tribes were also master woodworkers, creating elaborate totem poles and cedar-plank houses. In the north lived the tough survivors of the Arctic—the Inuit. They were skilled at hunting marine mammals, such as the polar bear, seal, walrus, narwhal, and beluga whale. But to survive the harsh winters of the north, the Inuit had to migrate to find caribou, Arctic char, and other food sources. Caribou were especially important: their fur and skins became the Inuit's winter clothing.

EARLY EUROPEAN VISITORS

Most historians agree the Vikings were the first nonnative explorers of Canada. Archaeologists found evidence of a permanent settlement in the eleventh century CE at L'Anse aux Meadows in Newfoundland. Leif Eriksson led a group of Viking settlers to Baffin Island and then traveled south to Newfoundland. While Leif returned home to Scandinavia, his brother Thorvald stayed and wintered on the land. Thorvald and his men attacked a group of aboriginals and were later killed.

But that would not be the last of the Vikings. In 1008 CE, Thorfinn Karlsefni went to Newfoundland with livestock, supplies, and 160 men.[1] The group settled at L'Anse aux Meadows and stayed for three years. The aboriginal people traded with the Vikings, but their interactions were never friendly. The Vikings eventually abandoned the settlement and returned home.

Leif Eriksson called Canada Vinland, or "wine land," for its wild grapes.

John Cabot's voyage from England began a new wave of European exploration and settlement in Canada.

EUROPEAN EXPLORERS AND COLONIES

In the fifteenth century, England sponsored John Cabot as its explorer to the New World. On June 24, 1497, John Cabot and his crew landed on Canadian shores. He claimed the land as the property of England. Cabot returned home shortly after his claim. He reported that the seas of the new land were teeming with cod, a fish prized in Europe. Cabot's tales brought fishermen to the coast, leading to contact with the aboriginal peoples. In the sixteenth century, the British made a few failed attempts to establish colonies in Canada.

Almost 40 years after Cabot, the French arrived in Canada. Jacques Cartier landed in 1534 and claimed land along the shores of the Saint Lawrence River, including Quebec, for France. His attempt at a colony in the early 1540s failed. It took more than 60 years for the French to attempt another colony. In 1608, French explorer Samuel de Champlain arrived and built a small settlement where Quebec City now stands. This was the start of a "New France" in North America. Soon more French would arrive. These settlers learned some of the methods of survival developed by the First Nations peoples, which undoubtedly helped them survive the harsh Canadian winters.

In 1610, English explorer Henry Hudson set out to find the Northwest Passage. It was believed

THE ACADIANS

In the seventeenth century, French settlers created a pastoral community in Nova Scotia, aiming to live harmoniously with the land. They called themselves the Acadie. By 1750, this small group had grown to approximately 14,000 residents.[2] The British, who claimed that land, believed the large French group to be a threat. The British rounded up and forced the Acadians to leave their community in 1755. Many were put on ships bound for Europe or the United States. The Cajuns of Louisiana in the southern United States are the descendants of some of the expelled Acadians.

this passage to Asia from Europe lay north of North America. Many explorers set out to find it. Hudson's crew sailed farther into Canada than anyone else, navigating the strait by Baffin Island and into Hudson and James Bays. The discovery of these bays would become vital to the fur trade, as they gave access to many inland waterways when not blocked by ice. However, the explorers found no passable northern water route from the Atlantic to the Pacific Ocean.

THE FUR TRADE

Beaver fur was big in the European fashion industry during the seventeenth century. The First Nations peoples knew how to trap the abundant animals, and Europeans traded goods—such as metal, firearms, ammunition, cloth, tobacco, and brandy—for the furs. But the furs were difficult to transport overland to coastal waters.

French explorers Pierre-Esprit Radisson and Médard Chouart des Groseilliers knew a route to Canada's interior was needed: Hudson Bay would be the key to the fur trade. They tried to get France to back them on this voyage to discover an inland route, but it was the British who would fund their expedition. The result was the Hudson's Bay Company (HBC), one of the first commercial companies in the world, established in 1670. The company, which exists today as a retail company, had a fur-trading monopoly for more than 100 years. The North West Company, established in 1783, later challenged HBC until the two companies joined in 1821.

Along with fur traders came missionaries. Jesuit missionaries from France first arrived in Quebec in 1625, bringing Roman Catholicism with them. In Europe, a religious struggle between Catholics and Protestants had long existed. The British were Protestants, and the French were Catholics. Missionaries sought to convert the First Nations bands to their religion. Thus the missionaries brought the Europeans' religious struggles to the New World.

CONFLICT AND TREATIES

The French, English, First Nations peoples, and Métis had established strongholds in different parts of the country. These communities were bound for conflict in their rapidly changing environment. Britain governed Newfoundland, Nova Scotia, and the Hudson Bay areas by 1713. And the French occupied the Saint Lawrence River and Great Lakes regions, extending down into the

THE TREATY OF UTRECHT

Signed in 1713, the Treaty of Utrecht relinquished France's claim to land in the Hudson Bay, Newfoundland, and Acadia regions to the British. But the treaty was not entirely effective. It did not define those areas around Hudson Bay, it gave France fishing rights in the waters off Newfoundland, and it provided unclear limits to the land in Acadia. It left many questions unanswered and fueled disputes, eventually leading to the Seven Years' War (1754–1763), usually called the French and Indian War in the United States.

FIRST NATIONS TREATIES

Starting in 1754, the British government began signing treaties with First Nations bands. Most of these treaties were agreements to sell native lands to the settlers. These treaties were rarely negotiated fairly, with aboriginals receiving small monetary payments for vast amounts of land.

modern-day United States. First Nations peoples were allies of either the British or the French.

The first of the major conflicts between the French and the British in the New World was part of the Seven Years' War. The Battle of the Plains of Abraham occurred on September 13, 1759, near Quebec. It ended badly for the French. The defeat basically ended French control of the area. The Treaty of Paris, signed in 1763, gave the British the rights to New France. British supremacy upset several First Nations bands, including the Ottawas, Ojibwas, Potawatomis, and Hurons. They led a rebellion, called Pontiac's War, against the British. Although this rebellion led the British to recognize certain aboriginal rights, the bands were largely unsuccessful and had weakened by August 1763. They signed the Niagara Treaty of 1764, promising peace between the First Nations and the British.

The relationship between the French and British was still strained. In 1774, the British government signed the Quebec Act. It gave rights to

Chief Pontiac and his allies visit Major Gladwyn of Britain during Pontiac's War in the 1760s.

the French in Quebec, promising the freedom to practice Catholicism and follow French civil law in the province. Then the American Revolution (1775–1783) began in the 13 British colonies along the East Coast of North America. When the colonists won independence from the British, thousands of British loyalists left the colonies and moved north toward Quebec, radically changing the province's culture. These loyalists were given aboriginal lands to farm, but they did not like living in pro-French conditions. This led to the Constitutional Act of 1791, which separated Quebec into Lower Canada (the current location of Quebec) and Upper Canada (where Ontario is today). Many British loyalists moved to Upper Canada and Nova Scotia. The aboriginals suffered, losing their rights in poorly negotiated treaties.

Things were not completely settled between the British and the newly formed United States. Skirmishes between Americans and aboriginal Canadians sprang up along the border between the countries, and the native bands appeared to be armed with British weapons. In the 1811 Battle of Tippecanoe, many bands formed an alliance and fought the Americans. The Americans won the battle, but they believed the British had incited the bands to action. In June 1812, the Americans declared war and invaded Canada. Meanwhile, the British were blocking trade with France and capturing American sailors. These factors led to the War of 1812. After many bloody battles between the British and the Americans and each side's native allies, neither side achieved a critical victory. The Treaty of Ghent was signed in 1814. It officially ended the conflict and settled the eastern boundary between the United States and the British territory of Canada.

CANADA GROWS

Throughout the late nineteenth century and into the twentieth, Canada grew at an incredible rate. After years of separate unsuccessful rebellions against British control, the four colonies were united under the British North America Act on July 1, 1867. Together they became known as the Dominion of Canada. A government was established, and Sir John A. Macdonald was named the country's first prime minister under the British crown. However, he wanted Canada to become more self-sufficient and less reliant on Britain.

The new government then purchased some land from the HBC. The land was home to many Métis people. Métis leader Louis Riel

Métis leader Louis Riel

led two uprisings, claiming the Métis had rights to the land. In 1870, the new province of Manitoba was created as part of a compromise. Some Métis settled in the province, but many moved west. In 1871, the province of British Columbia joined the dominion, as did Prince Edward Island on the eastern coast in 1873. The construction of the Canadian Pacific Railway, completed in 1885, contributed to Canada's growth. It ran across the entire country, uniting the provinces. The Yukon Territory was added in 1898, and in 1905, Saskatchewan and Alberta became part of the dominion.

In the 20 years after 1841, Canada's population rose from 1.1 million to 2.5 million.[3] Much of this population boom was due to immigration. One group of immigrants were Irish who had fled Ireland to escape the potato famine. Other immigrants were African Americans who escaped slavery in the United States through the Underground Railroad. Immigration peaked in 1913, just before World War I (1914–1918).

THE KLONDIKE GOLD RUSH

On August 17, 1896, gold was found near where the Klondike and Yukon Rivers meet in western Yukon. By the next year, approximately 30,000 prospectors had come to the area in search of gold.[4] Many died from malnutrition, avalanches, and hypothermia. By 1899, the gold rush wound down in the Klondike as prospectors instead went to Alaska to seek their fortunes.

WARS AND THE GREAT DEPRESSION

Canada's military was first tested in the Boer War (1899–1902) in South Africa. When Britain decided to go to war, the Canadian military supported their king by joining in. Its next test was World War I. The Canadian military again joined the fight, despite opposition among French Canadians. Several Canadians were recognized as war heroes. At the Second Battle of Ypres in 1915, Canadian troops successfully held off German troops. But Canada achieved its greatest military triumph at Vimy Ridge in 1917. The troops fought the Germans under difficult conditions but seized the ridge, which had been a solid stronghold for the Germans.

After World War I, Canada was internationally recognized as an independent country. It was given a vote and a say in the peace negotiations after the war. In 1931, Britain officially granted Canada greater autonomy by passing the Statute of Westminster. Around this time, the Great Depression that had started in the United States was affecting Canada even more severely. Drought hit the prairies, and farms failed. People were unemployed, and it was a difficult time for many.

World War II (1939–1945) brought Canada out of the Great Depression. Canada entered the war on September 10, 1939. Industry in Canada boomed as the country produced equipment needed in the war. Despite heavy casualties—including 42,000 killed—Canada emerged triumphantly.[5] The country became one of the founding members of the United Nations (UN) and the North Atlantic Treaty Organization

JAPANESE-CANADIAN INTERNMENT

During World War II, after Japan bombed Pearl Harbor, the Canadian government ordered Japanese Canadians to be moved from their homes and placed in internment camps. This action paralleled actions taken in the United States after the attack. It was believed people of Japanese descent would assist Japan in further attacks against the United States or Canada. More than 22,000 Japanese Canadians were interned in the camps, although no Japanese Canadian was charged with disloyalty to Canada.[6] While at the camps, the land and property of the Japanese Canadians were sold. On September 22, 1988, Canadian prime minister Brian Mulroney officially acknowledged that Japanese Canadians had been unfairly treated during the war and offered them a monetary settlement.

(NATO). It was the beginning of a new era.

THE BIRTH OF MODERN CANADA

After the war, the Great Depression was over, and financial stability returned. In 1949, Newfoundland joined the Canadian dominion. A liberal internationalist outlook was adopted for the country, led by Prime Minister Louis Saint Laurent and Secretary of State for External Affairs Lester Pearson. Pearson went on to become prime minister, and he also won the Nobel Peace Prize in 1957 for helping resolve the Suez Crisis in the Middle East.

In 1950, Canada contributed military forces to help UN troops defend South Korea against invasion from North Korea. The 1960s saw the birth of Medicare in Canada. This public health-care system guaranteed medical care to all people in Canada. The Medical Care Act was introduced in 1966, and by 1972 all provinces had Medicare programs. This was just one of many social programs instituted in the country at this time.

By the 1960s, many French Canadians desired more official recognition within the government. Two important leaders in the events were Prime Minister Pierre Trudeau and Premier René Lévesque of Québec. During this time, the French-Canadian terrorist group Front de Libération du Québec (FLQ) formed. In 1970, the FLQ kidnapped British trade commissioner James Cross and Quebec labour minister Pierre Laporte. The police rescued Cross, but Laporte was found murdered. Trudeau sent military troops to Québec and banned the FLQ. He continued to work for a united Canada and resisted claims of Quebec sovereignty. But in 1980, Lévesque campaigned for a referendum for an independent Quebec. The majority voted against this, but it still had many supporters.

The British North America Act of 1867 had provided a constitution for the Dominion of Canada. In 1982, the Charter of Rights and Freedoms was added to the Canadian Constitution. The Constitution Act of 1982 transferred all legal powers over Canada from the United Kingdom to the Canadian government. Among its many features, the new Constitution also officially set the bilingual policy, outlined the process to amend the constitution, and set certain aboriginal rights. The province of Quebec, however, refused to recognize the charter. In 1984, Brian Mulroney became the prime minister and worked to reform the constitutional system. The Meech Lake Accord in 1987 aimed to recognize Quebec as a distinct society within Canada, but it fell just short of acceptance from all the provinces by 1990 and did not go into effect. Mulroney tried again with the Charlottetown Accord in 1992, which dealt with Quebec sovereignty issues and aboriginal self-government, but it was also rejected by popular vote. On April 1, 1999, Canada established its newest territory of Nunavut, previously part of the Northwest Territories. It became a homeland for the Inuit.

By 2012, many of the constitutional reforms were in place. Quebec had achieved official recognition for its French heritage in 2006, federal and provincial governments were making new agreements with many First Nations bands, and the Inuit people were the majority within Nunavut.

Inuit elder Ekalool Juralak marks the 1999 creation of the territory and government of Nunavut by lighting a traditional oil lamp.

CHAPTER 5

PEOPLE:
A CULTURAL MOSAIC

With their variety of cultures, ethnicities, and languages, the diversity of the Canadian people defines modern Canada. The largest ethnic groups remain the French, British, and other Europeans, with the First Nations peoples next, and lastly a variety of non-European immigrants and mixed-race peoples.

Canada's official government policy of "multiculturalism within a bilingual framework" epitomizes Canadians' tolerant attitude.[1] The country's people are a cultural mosaic, and its culture is a collection of distinct differences, not one blended identity. This attitude developed mostly because of the struggles of French Canadians to maintain their culture in a British country. They succeeded and paved the way for other cultures to maintain their identities in Canada. That is why Canada has two official languages: English and French. And there are

Quebec City celebrates its French heritage with a monument to Samuel de Champlain, the city's founder.

SAINT LAURENT BOULEVARD

In some Canadian cities, people need to switch languages when they cross the street! This is the case with Saint Laurent Boulevard, also called "the Main," in Montreal. It is the physical division between the city's east and west. West of the Main is predominantly English speaking, while east is predominantly French speaking.

approximately 100 more unofficial languages spoken in the country, including many native languages.[2] In Nunavut and the Northwest Territories, various aboriginal languages are the official languages.

Canada is home to approximately 34,300,083 people, ranking the country's population at thirty-fifth in the world. The vast majority of Canadians live within 100 miles (160 km) of the United States, where Canada's urban centers are located. Of the entire population, 81 percent live in urban areas.[3] Within those urban areas, each square mile is crowded with 635 people (245 people per sq km). Toronto is the most populous city. In the north, there are just 7 people per square mile (2.7 people per sq km) in an area that contains 40 percent of Canada's land.[4] The high population density in cities forces the many cultures of Canada to interact with one another and find harmonious ways to live together. Outside of the cities, much of the country is uninhabited.

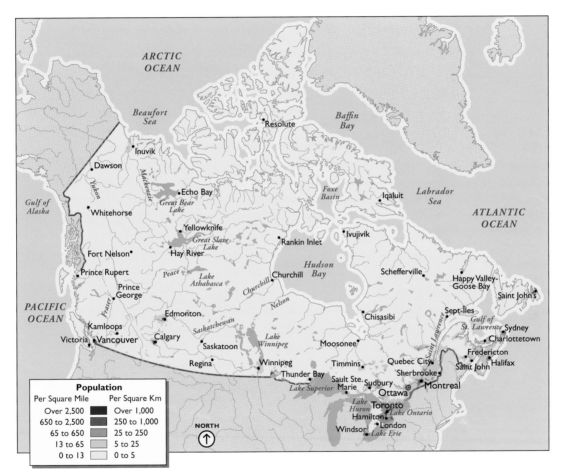

Population Density of Canada

Legend — Population

Per Square Mile	Per Square Km
Over 2,500	Over 1,000
650 to 2,500	250 to 1,000
65 to 650	25 to 250
13 to 65	5 to 25
0 to 13	0 to 5

NORTH

Map labels: ARCTIC OCEAN, Beaufort Sea, Resolute, Baffin Bay, Inuvik, Dawson, Echo Bay, Foxe Basin, Iqaluit, Labrador Sea, Gulf of Alaska, Whitehorse, Great Bear Lake, ATLANTIC OCEAN, Yukon, Mackenzie, Yellowknife, Great Slave Lake, Rankin Inlet, Ivujivik, Fort Nelson, Hay River, Hudson Bay, Scheffervile, Happy Valley-Goose Bay, Prince Rupert, Peace, Lake Athabasca, Churchill, Churchill, Saint John's, Prince George, Nelson, Sept-Îles, Gulf of St. Lawrence, Sydney, Edmonton, Chisasibi, Fraser, Saskatchewan, PACIFIC OCEAN, Kamloops, Lake Winnipeg, Moosonee, Charlottetown, Victoria, Vancouver, Calgary, Saskatoon, Saint Lawrence, Fredericton, Regina, Winnipeg, Timmins, Quebec City, Saint John, Halifax, Thunder Bay, Sherbrooke, Sault Ste. Marie, Sudbury, Montreal, Lake Superior, Ottawa, Toronto, Lake Huron, Hamilton, Lake Ontario, Windsor, London, Lake Erie

MANY CULTURES, ONE LAND

More than 200 ethnic groups live in Canada.[5] Those of British ancestry make up the largest group, with 28 percent of the total population. They are concentrated in Ontario and the eastern provinces. French Canadians make up the next-largest group at 23 percent.[6] Quebec is the center of the French-Canadian population, but some also live in British Columbia and New Brunswick.

People of other European origins make up another 15 percent of the total population.[7] The numbers of Italian, Ukrainian, Dutch, German, and Greek Canadians are especially large. Many Ukrainians settled in the provinces of the prairies, while Dutch settlers chose the farmlands of southern Ontario. Many German speakers live in Lunenburg in Nova Scotia and Kitchener-Waterloo in Ontario. And Toronto, Montreal, and Vancouver have "Little Italy" and Greek neighborhoods.

BRITISH HOME CHILDREN

Between 1869 and the late 1940s, British philanthropic and religious organizations brought approximately 100,000 British children—or Home Children, as they were called—to Canada to live with Canadian families and work as farm laborers or domestic servants.[8] Many of these children came from urban slums and were under the age of 14. Sending them to Canada released the British government from taking care of the children. For Canadian families, the children were an unpaid labor force.

YOU SAY IT!

English	French	Inuktitut
Good Morning/Good Day	Bonjour (bohn-ZHOOR)	Ullaakkut (oo-LAH-coot)
Good-bye	Au revoir (oh ruh-VWAHR)	Tavvauvutit (tah-VOW-voo-teet)
Yes	Oui (WEE)	Ii (EE)
No	Non (NOHN)	Aagga (AH-gah)
I am hungry.	J'ai faim (zhay FAM)	Kaaktunga (KAHK-toon-gah)
I don't understand.	Je ne comprends pas (zhu nu kahm-prahnd PAH)	Tukisinngittunga (Too-kih-sihn-GIH-toon-gah)

The First Nations peoples represent 2 percent of the population.[9] When Métis and Inuit are added to this group, their total population is more than 1 million.[10] The largest of the native groups are people of Cree descent, who number approximately 120,000.[11] More than 60 languages are spoken within the more than 630 First Nations communities. They fall into ten distinct language families: Algonquian, Athabascan, Siouan, Salish, Tsimshian, Wakashan, Iroquoian, Haida, Kutenai, and Tlingit.[12] There are more than 2,250 reserves set aside by the government for the people of the First Nations.[13] The Inuit live in the far north of Nunavut (not a reserve), Labrador, and northern Quebec. Aboriginal and Métis peoples also live in urban areas of Canada.

Six percent of Canada's population is of Asian, African, or Arab descent.[14] Asians are an especially large, and growing, part of the Canadian population. Chinese Canadians are the largest non-European and nonnative ethnic group, with a population of more than 1 million.[15] Most Chinese immigrants live in Toronto or Vancouver. East Indians are another large ethnic group concentrated in these two cities. Many were born in India, but some also come from Guyana, East Africa, Bangladesh, Sri Lanka, or Pakistan. People of African descent come to Canada from Africa or the Caribbean, but some are the descendants of American slaves who escaped to Canada. Most African Canadians

Nunavut means "our land" in Inuktitut, a dialect of the Inuit.

Chinese Canadians make up the largest ethnic group after European and aboriginal Canadians.

Canadians of all ages and races gather in Ottawa to celebrate Canada Day.

live in Ontario, Quebec, British Columbia, and Alberta. The mixed-race population is large at 26 percent.[16] This number has been rapidly growing over the past decades.

Approximately 68.5 percent of Canadians are between the ages of 15 and 64, with 15.7 percent younger than 14 and 15.9 percent older than 65. Women live a bit longer than men, with an average life expectancy of 84 years. Men live an average of 79 years. Between both sexes, the average person lives approximately 81.5 years, ranking Canada twelfth in the world for life expectancy.[17]

JOHN MURRAY GIBBON

John Murray Gibbon was a prolific Canadian author with a deep interest in the culture of Canada. His 1938 book *Canadian Mosaic: The Making of a Northern Nation* influenced the country's government in its policies of multiculturalism. In 1954, the Canadian government recognized Gibbon as a Person of National Historic Significance.

RELIGIOUS DIVERSITY

The French and their missionaries brought Roman Catholicism to Canada. Today, Roman Catholics make up the largest religious group at 42.6 percent of Canada's population. The other major religion is Protestantism, brought to Canada by the British. It includes the United Church, Anglican, Baptist, and Lutheran denominations and makes up 23.3 percent of the population.[18]

Muslims are a growing segment in Canada and are currently at 2 percent of the population.[19] The numbers of Hindus, Buddhists, and Sikhs have also been on the rise. Each religion represents approximately 1 percent of the population. At almost 2 percent are people of the Christian Orthodox religion, and people of the Jewish faith are 1 percent of the total.[20] At least 16 percent of Canadians are not affiliated with any faith.[21]

THE FIRST BUDDHIST TEMPLE IN CANADA

By 1905, many people of Japanese descent were living in British Columbia. These Japanese Canadians were Buddhist and wanted their own place of worship, but only Anglican and Methodist churches existed in the area. Japanese Buddhists were afraid their community would lose its faith without a place to worship. They raised $5,668 in donations and opened the first Buddhist temple in Canada on December 12, 1905.[22]

The traditional beliefs of the First Nations and Inuit peoples are based on elaborate ceremonies, mythology, and social customs that honor the sacred and supernatural. Religious ceremonies and customs vary greatly throughout the country, but three main myths are found in their group of religions. Creation myths explain the creation of the cosmos. Trickster myths feature the Transformer

Muslim women in Toronto demonstrate against Israeli occupation of Gaza.

character, who steals things, such as light or animals, and sets them loose to change the world. Culture hero myths feature the Transformer as a human being who has special powers and performs heroic feats. Special ceremonies are performed for deaths, births, and initiations. The spiritual leaders of the First Nations are called shamans.

The Inuit and Métis peoples prefer not to be called First Nations.

Other religious communities throughout Canada include the Mennonites, Amish, and Hutterites. Mennonites originated in Germany and now live in both urban and rural areas of Canada. Approximately 191,000 Mennonites live in Canada.[23] Cities with the largest Mennonite populations are Winnipeg, Vancouver, Saskatoon, and Kitchener-Waterloo. This religion emphasizes separation from the world and nonconformity with mainstream society. Mennonites have created their own schools and organizations to teach and encourage their religious and social beliefs. The Amish settled in southwestern Ontario, where they live simple lives without using modern technology. They speak a German dialect. The Hutterites mostly live in Manitoba, Saskatchewan, and Alberta. Their rural communities are based around agriculture. They believe in communal living, communal property, nonviolence, and adult baptism. They have kept the dress, customs, and language of their German ancestors.

Drums are an essential part of many Inuit ceremonies.

CHAPTER 6

CULTURE: IN CONSTANT EVOLUTION

Separate cultures define the Canadian identity. Many of these cultural pockets have grown from the first French, British, and aboriginal settlements. They continue to grow and expand as immigrants arrive from around the world. This makes for a national culture as varied and beautiful as the Canadian landscape itself.

But if there is one truly unifying force in Canada, it is ice hockey. The game was invented in Canada, and it is a national passion and the country's official winter sport. Hockey rinks can be found in almost every town. Kids are taught to play at an early age, some just after they begin

The first hockey puck was used in Ontario in 1860.

Goaltender Roberto Luongo took a victory lap after the Canadian men's ice hockey team won gold in the 2010 Winter Olympics.

walking. The Canadian $5 bill pays homage to the sport. Even Canadian prime minister Stephen Harper is obsessed with hockey: he is writing a book on the early history of Canadian hockey. Canadian authors Bruce Kidd and John Macfarlane wrote that hockey is "the dance of life, an affirmation that despite the deathly chill of winter we are alive."[1]

Wayne Gretzky is probably the most well-known Canadian hockey player of all time. He rose to fame in Canada but ended his hockey days in the United States. Gretzky had a record-breaking career, and many believe he is the best hockey player in the history of the sport. Canada also contributed the first female National Hockey League (NHL) player, Manon Rhéaume. She was the backup goalie for the Nashville Knights. Canadian hockey players are found on many US teams. In 2012, more than half of NHL players and seven NHL teams were Canadian.[2]

WAYNE GRETZKY

Born in Brantford, Ontario, Wayne Gretzky had hockey in his blood from birth. He was obsessed by the time he was six, so his dad built a rink in their backyard where Gretzky could practice. He first started playing in leagues when he was six and never stopped until he went pro. He played professional hockey for 20 years before retiring.

SPORTS AND THE OUTDOORS

Lacrosse is Canada's official summer sport. This team sport uses a rubber ball and sticks with nets at one end. The sport originated with First Nations bands in Upper Canada. Some other popular sports in Canada are baseball, Canadian football, basketball, and golf.

With its many mountains and cold climate, Canada is the perfect place for skiing, snowboarding, snowmobiling, and enjoying other winter sports. Whistler Blackcomb outside of Vancouver is thought to be the best ski resort in all of North America. Canada is also a fishing paradise. Salmon, smallmouth bass, walleye, and northern pike are just some of the sport fish that swim in Canadian waters. They can be found in Canada's many national parks, where hiking, camping, canoeing, and white-water rafting are also popular activities.

ARTS AND CRAFTS

Aboriginal crafts in Canada range from the traditional Mi'kmaq baskets of Lennox Island to the beautifully carved totem poles of British Columbia. Native sculptor Bill Reid was one of Canada's greatest artists. His work was chosen to appear on the Canadian $20 bill. The Inuit construct stone figures called *inuksuit*. Stones are placed on other stones to build a humanlike figure. Nunavut's flag features an inuksuk. The inuksuk was also chosen as the official logo of the 2010 Winter Olympics,

Inuksuit are traditionally used for navigation or to mark important places such as hunting grounds.

which were held in Vancouver. Crafts from the colonial times of Canada's past include *ceinture fléchée*, a type of weaving from Quebec in which weavers use their fingers instead of a loom. It was used to make sashes worn by French-Canadian explorers. Traditional hooked mats are made in Newfoundland and Labrador. English immigrants brought this craft to Canada.

The country's wild landscape and native peoples were the subjects of classically trained painters in Canada. Some early painters were Robert Field and Antoine Plamondon. They trained in the late eighteenth century and early nineteenth century in Europe and brought their artistic skills to Canada. The first well-known, Canadian-trained painters were Homer Watson and Ozias Leduc. The Group of Seven was a group of modern painters who joined together in the 1920s. They wanted to produce some new and distinctly Canadian paintings, focusing on landscapes. The artists in this group were Franklin Carmichael, Lawren Harris, A. Y. Jackson, Frank Johnston, Arthur Lismer, J. E. H. MacDonald, and F. H. Varley. The group experimented with new painting techniques and color usage, daring to veer from the classical style of painting revered up until that time.

General Idea was a multimedia collaboration of modern artists who assumed the names AA Bronson, Felix Partz, and Jorge Zontal. They focused on interpreting and understanding pop culture. Michael Snow is another modern artist who works in multiple mediums. One

An inuksuk perches atop Whistler Mountain in British Columbia, Canada.

of his famous works was an installation of 48 holographic images. Internationally famous modern artist Janet Cardiff creates audio and video installations.

ARCHITECTURE

Canada's earliest structures were built by First Nations peoples. They included igloos, tepees, wigwams, and longhouses. From the seventeenth century on, structures built by early explorers and missionaries included impressive cathedrals and chapels. One example is the neo-Gothic Notre-Dame Basilica of Montreal, completed in 1829. Chateaus, such as the Château Frontenac in Quebec, dot the Canadian countryside.

Canada is also known for its tall structures, including the CN Tower in Toronto, which stands 1,815 feet (553 m) tall.[3] Modern architect Ludwig Mies van der Rohe designed a gas station on Nuns' Island,

CULTURAL PRESERVATION

Approximately 2 percent of the Canadian government's budget is set aside for cultural preservation.[4] These funds subsidize the Canadian film and television industry to encourage a more uniquely Canadian culture. They also support other art organizations, such as the National Ballet Company, as well as individual artists.

The interior of the Notre-Dame Basilica of Montreal

Montreal, which was built in 1969 and recently renovated. It has a sleek, ultramodern style. One of the most famous architects in the modern world, Frank Gehry, is from Toronto. He uses materials in new and expressive ways to form buildings that look almost fluid. One of his most famous buildings is the Guggenheim Museum in Bilbao, Spain.

MUSIC AND DANCE

Neil Young, Justin Bieber, Leonard Cohen, and Celine Dion are just a few of the famous musicians who hail from Canada. Deadmau5, also known as Joel Thomas Zimmerman, is one of the hottest electronic acts in the world, playing at huge music festivals including Coachella in Indio, California. Canadian crooner Michael Bublé is known for his versions of swing-era classics and other ballads. Canadians Avril Lavigne and Alanis Morissette are two internationally famous female pop singers. And Glenn Gould was a world-renowned classical pianist from Toronto.

Canada's major cities boast talented orchestras. The country also has three professional ballet companies: the National Ballet Company, Royal Winnipeg Ballet, and Les Grands Ballets Canadiens. The Canadian Opera Company is one of the largest in North America and shares the Four Seasons Centre for the Performing Arts building with the National Ballet Company. Numerous music festivals are held in Canada, two of

Canadian sensation Justin Bieber performs in New York City's Rockefeller Plaza.

its most famous being the Montreal International Jazz Festival and the Edmonton Folk Music Festival.

LITERATURE, TELEVISION, AND FILM

The earliest Canadian literature was written in French by explorers, missionaries, and settlers. In the late nineteenth to early twentieth centuries, authors such as William Kirby and Mazo de la Roche wrote works that have become classics. Lucy Maud Montgomery wrote the world-famous *Anne of Green Gables* series for young adults. The first book was published in 1908. In the 1940s, French writer Germaine Guèvremont wrote *The Outlanders*, making her a famous French-language novelist. Some contemporary authors include Margaret Atwood, who wrote *The Handmaid's Tale*; Alice Munro, who writes short stories; and Michael Ondaatje, who wrote *The English Patient*.

ANNE: BIG IN JAPAN

Anne of Green Gables is a novel about a red-haired orphan girl who is sent to live with two elderly siblings on Prince Edward Island. The novel has become beloved around the world. But in Japan, Anne has somewhat of a cult following. The country built a theme park called Canadian World in Hokkaido to celebrate Anne and nineteenth-century Canada. Thousands of Japanese tourists also visit Prince Edward Island each year to see the setting of the *Anne of Green Gables* book.

The Green Gables farm on Prince Edward Island was the real-life inspiration for the setting of *Anne of Green Gables*.

Canada has several television networks, but most Canadians watch shows from the United States. Cable television is extremely popular among Canadians. The Canadian Broadcasting Corporation (CBC) operates radio and television in both French and English. *Hockey Night in Canada* is a popular show on the CBC. There are also two big privately owned television stations: Canadian Television (CTV) for English speakers and *Réseau de Télévision* (TVA) for French speakers.

Canada also has a thriving film industry. Filmmakers Jason and Ivan Reitman, James Cameron, and Nia Vardalos are Canadians. Some other famous actors and directors are David Cronenberg, Ryan Gosling, Jim Carrey, Anna Paquin, and Rachel McAdams. Toronto is a huge film-producing center and also hosts the Toronto International Film Festival every year.

HOLIDAYS AND FESTIVALS

Canada has nine national holidays, including Christmas, Thanksgiving, and Labour Day. Canada Day on July 1 marks the union of provinces into the nation of Canada. This day is celebrated with fireworks, parades, and the singing of the national anthem, "O Canada." On June 24, the Fête Nationale du Québec is celebrated to mark the summer solstice and honor Jean Baptiste, the patron saint of French Canadians. This is not a national holiday, but it is a big one in the province of Québec. It is celebrated with bonfires, music, and Catholic mass.

A three-day, 150-mile (240 km) dogsled race is the highlight of the Caribou Carnival.

Festivals include the Caribou Carnival, which takes place in March and is held in Yellowknife. The Stratford Shakespeare Festival, held in May, hosts many theatrical performances. Montreal's Just for Laughs comedy festival is held in July. And the Quebec Winter Carnival, held from late January to February, is a huge winter celebration.

Canada Day festivities on the lawn in front of British Columbia's parliament building

CANADIAN DISHES

Canada's top dining districts are Toronto, Montreal, and Vancouver, but from coast to coast each area boasts its own specialties. Seafood is excellent along the coasts. There is fine French dining in Quebec. And in the central provinces, beef and game are big, as are freshwater fish. Pierogi, or stuffed Ukrainian dumplings, are also popular. Saskatoons, berries native to Canada, are used in pies and jams. Some native dishes include halibut stew, dried caribou, and bannock, a pan-fried bread. Uniquely Canadian foods include Canadian back bacon, *tourtière* (a meat pie with a pastry crust), and the Nanaimo bar (a layered desert bar). Beer is also big in Canada. A popular Canadian beer is from Molson, the oldest brewery in North America. Maple syrup is one of the most famous Canadian foods.

Canada makes 85 percent of the world's maple syrup.

Sugar shacks across Canada produce the finest maple syrup.

CHAPTER 7

POLITICS: BRITISH BASIS AND CANADIAN GOALS

Canada began as a land of two empires: the British and the French. This tie is evident in the country's modern political structure and in one of its most controversial political issues—Quebec sovereignty. The political structure is symbolically tied with the British monarchy and modeled after the British political system. The separatist issue is part of French Canadians' desire to maintain a distinctly French culture. It has come to the forefront of Canadian politics several times in the past, and it is still far from being resolved. It seems the British and French cultures will always shape Canada's politics and government.

Queen Elizabeth II and Prime Minister Stephen Harper were Canada's leaders in 2012.

Canada is a constitutional monarchy and a parliamentary democracy with a federal political system. The federal government has three main branches: the executive, the legislative, and the judicial branches.

EXECUTIVE BRANCH

The head of state and leader of the executive branch—only in title—is the reigning monarch of the United Kingdom, which in 2012 was Queen Elizabeth II. In Canada, a governor-general represents the monarch. This person is a Canadian who is recommended by the prime minister and appointed by the monarch. He or she has no fixed term but usually serves for five years. The 2012 governor-general was David Johnston. These two members of the executive branch do not have the power to make laws or govern directly.

The third member of the executive branch is the prime minister.

THE GOVERNOR-GENERAL

The mainly ceremonial duties held by the Canadian governor-general include the following:

• summoning, opening, and ending sessions of Parliament

• reading a speech at the opening of the Parliamentary session

• giving final approval for bills passed by the House of Commons and Senate to become law

• signing state documents

• dissolving Parliament for an election

• appointing the prime minister, Supreme Court justices, cabinet ministers, and senators

This person is an elected member of the House of Commons and also the head of government. The Canadian prime minister is not directly elected in a nationwide election. He or she is elected to the House of Commons. The political party with the most members in the House of Commons is considered to be in power. The governor-general asks the leader of that political party to be the prime minister. The 2012 prime minister was Conservative Party leader Stephen Harper. Reporting to the prime minister is his or her cabinet. The prime minister chooses cabinet members from the members of Parliament. Each cabinet member is put in charge of a part of the government, such as agriculture, the environment, or national defense.

PRIME MINISTER STEPHEN HARPER

On February 6, 2006, Stephen Harper was sworn in as Canada's twenty-second prime minister. Harper was the first Conservative to gain power after 13 years with the Liberal Party in control. In 2012, Harper was serving his third term as prime minister, with a main focus on the economy.

LEGISLATIVE BRANCH

Parliament consists of two branches: the House of Commons and the Senate. The House of Commons is made up of elected members and has more power than the Senate. There are 308 seats in the House of

Commons, although this number was scheduled to increase to 338 in 2015. Members are elected to their positions in proportion to the population of each province. Canadians vote for individual candidates, often according to which political party they represent. The prime minister recommends senators to the governor-general, who then appoints them to the Senate. There are 105 Senate members. The Senate considers and most often ratifies bills that have passed through the House of Commons. The Senate also investigates and reports on public issues and concerns, such as aboriginal affairs and human rights. Both the Senate and the House of Commons have Speakers. The Speakers are the presiding officers of each legislative body.

Elected officials generally serve through the next election, and under normal circumstances, elections are held every four years. If the prime minister is defeated in an election, the governor-general appoints a new prime minister.

Within each province or territory is a provincial legislature headed by an elected premier. The monarch is represented by a lieutenant-governor. Representatives from each of these provincial legislatures work in the federal parliament. The provincial legislatures have power to make laws affecting provincial matters, such as natural resources in the province or penalties for breaking provincial laws.

> **Parliament Hill attracts more than 1.5 million visitors each year.**

Parliament Hill in Ottawa is the seat of Canada's legislature.

The Canadian flag

LEGAL SYSTEM AND JUDICIAL BRANCH

There is a common-law system in all of Canada except for Quebec, which follows the French civil code. The common-law system is based on British common law. Common law allows courts to make decisions based on previous court rulings. In general, the French civil code relies on broad, general principles, leaving court cases up to wider interpretation.

Both the common law and civil code systems in Canada must adhere to the country's constitution.

The Canadian judicial system has four layers of courts. On the lowest level are the provincial and territorial courts. They hear cases involving federal and provincial laws. The next level has the provincial or territorial superior courts. These courts try the most serious criminal and civil cases, such as divorce and cases involving large amounts of money. In Nunavut, these two levels of courts are combined into the Nunavut Court of Justice.

Also at this level is the Federal Court, which can deal only with cases concerning federal law. Above this level are the courts of appeal, both federal and provincial or territorial. Specialized courts include the Tax Court of Canada and the Military Courts. The highest court is the Supreme Court of Canada. It is the final court of appeal for all the lower courts. It has jurisdiction over constitutional, civil, administrative, and criminal law.

CANADA'S FLAG

On February 15, 1965, Canada introduced its new flag. It has a red maple leaf centered on a white background. Along the sides are red stripes. The maple leaf has been a Canadian symbol since 1700. In 1921, red and white became Canada's official colors.

THE CANADIAN CONSTITUTION

The Canadian constitution was established in 1867 with the British North America Act, which was later renamed the Constitution Act of 1867. It created a federation that initially consisted of four provinces, set up the legal system, and established French and English as the official languages of the country. A major change was made with the Constitution Act of 1982. This act transferred control over the constitution from Britain to Canada, added the Charter of Rights and Freedoms, set out the rights of aboriginal peoples, and created procedures for amending the constitution.

STRUCTURE OF THE GOVERNMENT OF CANADA

Executive Branch	Legislative Branch	Judicial Branch
Monarch Governor-General Prime Minister Cabinet	Senate House of Commons	Supreme Court Federal Court of Canada Provincial Courts Tax Court Military Court

POLITICAL PARTIES

Canada has five major political parties. They are the Bloc Québécois, Conservative Party of Canada, Green Party, Liberal Party, and New Democratic Party. The Bloc Québécois is dedicated to the sovereignty of Quebec and protecting its rights. The Conservative Party is in favor of smaller government, lower taxes, and more provincial power. The Green Party is focused on nonviolence, ecologically safe practices, social justice, and fair trade. The Liberal Party is the oldest party in Canada and works for deficit reduction, balanced budgets, renewable energy, and equal rights. And the New Democratic Party favors environmental protection, equality, poverty reduction, and higher corporate taxes. The party in control in 2012 was the

"Whereas Canada is founded upon principles that recognize the supremacy of God and the rule of law:

1. The Canadian Charter of Rights and Freedoms guarantees the rights and freedoms set out in it subject only to such reasonable limits prescribed by law as can be demonstrably justified in a free and democratic society.

2. Everyone has the following fundamental freedoms:

(a) freedom of conscience and religion;

(b) freedom of thought, belief, opinion, and expression, including freedom of the press and other media of communication;

(c) freedom of peaceful assembly; and

(d) freedom of association."[1]

—*Excerpt from the Canadian Charter of Rights and Freedoms*

Conservative Party. So far, only the Conservative and Liberal parties have formed governments.

CURRENT POLITICAL CHALLENGES

Economic policy is the primary issue, with Canada still struggling to recover from the global recession that began in 2008. Immigration policy is another issue in Canadian politics. Some advocate for limiting immigration, while others want open borders. The federal government encourages immigration for economic growth.

Some political issues relate to the rights of First Nations peoples. Land claims are in constant debate with the government. As native peoples were relocated in the country, certain land rights were promised to them, but the government did not always keep their promises. Hunting and fishing rights are also issues for the First Nations peoples.

The question of Quebec is another ongoing issue. Some argue it should become a separate nation

THE ASSEMBLY OF FIRST NATIONS

The Assembly of First Nations is an intertribal organization formed in 1982. It lobbies for political recognition of the First Nations bands within the federal government of Canada. The organization also advocates for treaty rights, land claims, and economic development. The group was involved with the establishment of Nunavut in 1999. It continues to be an influential organization in Canadian politics.

College students in Montreal, Quebec, stage a demonstration against a law that restricts students' right to protest.

from the federation of Canada. In 2006, the federal government declared Quebec was a nation inside a united Canada. The province continues to raise issues concerning its rights as the only predominantly French region of Canada.

Canada's universal health-care system is another hotly debated issue. The debate centers on its high cost. Rising costs in health care have caused the government to limit what is covered. And health care is unevenly distributed in the country. While Ontario has excellent health-care services, the Northwest Territories do not. Health-care funding needs to be increased to keep the system updated and equal throughout the country.

Other important issues facing the country include climate change and other environmental issues, reforming parliament, international relations, and defense and security.

CHAPTER 8

ECONOMICS: AN AFFLUENT COUNTRY

Canada is an affluent country with a high standard of living. The per capita income is $41,100, ranking it twentieth in the world, although 9.4 percent of its people still live below the poverty line. Canada ranks fifteenth in the world in gross domestic product (GDP).[1] And the *United Nations Human Development Report* ranks Canada as sixth of the world's best places to live out of 187 countries.[2] The country's abundant natural resources brought early explorers there centuries ago. These rich resources drove Canada's development. The country has since evolved a capitalist, free-market economy that closely resembles that of the United States. The Canadian dollar is strong, trading at almost the equivalent of the US dollar.

The largest trees in Canada grow on the western coast.

Timber is one of Canada's most abundant and important natural resources.

NAFTA

The North American Free Trade Agreement (NAFTA) was signed by Canada, the United States, and Mexico in 1994. With this agreement, the three countries could freely trade products without the restrictions of tariffs. Since the agreement, Canada's exports to the United States have increased dramatically. Canada also imports more goods from Mexico and the United States than it did before NAFTA.

Trade is an important aspect of the Canadian economy. Canada's biggest trade partner is the United States, with the United Kingdom coming in second.[3] Other important trading partners include China, Japan, Mexico, and Germany. Canada has many products and services to trade with the world. Services make up the largest portion of the GDP, with industry second and agriculture third.

AGRICULTURE, FORESTRY, HUNTING, AND FISHING

Crops can be grown on only one-twelfth of Canada's land.[4] The Prairie Provinces are ideal for agriculture, especially grain crops. This industry employs only 2 percent of the labor force, but it produces large amounts of food for Canadians and for export.[5] Its products include wheat, tobacco, oilseeds, fruits, vegetables, soybeans, grain corn, and white beans. Farmers also raise livestock and dairy cows.

Forests cover half of Canada's land and have become one of the country's most important resources.[6] As many as 250 million trees are felled in a successful year. Lumber, newsprint, and pulp are some of the industry's major products. Canada is the world's lead exporter of newsprint and pulp, which is mostly sold to the United States. But Canada's forests are being depleted faster than they can be replenished. And this industry is subject to the threats of fire, insects, and disease. It is important that this industry be sustainably managed because it is the country's largest employer. In 2012, approximately 300,000 Canadian jobs were directly related to the production of wood and wood products. Another 700,000 jobs were indirectly related to but dependent on forestry.[7]

The hunting industry led to the development of Canada. Restrictions on the fur trade are currently in place to protect the country's wildlife, but fur continues to be one of Canada's exports to the world. Overfishing and pollution have depleted fish resources in Canada. Yet with rich coastal waters off the Atlantic and Pacific coasts, Canada is still a lead exporter of fish products.

MINERALS AND ENERGY

Large deposits of minerals can be found on the Canadian Shield, the Western Cordillera, and the Appalachians. The country is a world leader in the production of uranium, zinc, nickel, potash, asbestos, sulfur,

Off the southeastern coast of Newfoundland and Labrador lie 1,345 million barrels of oil.

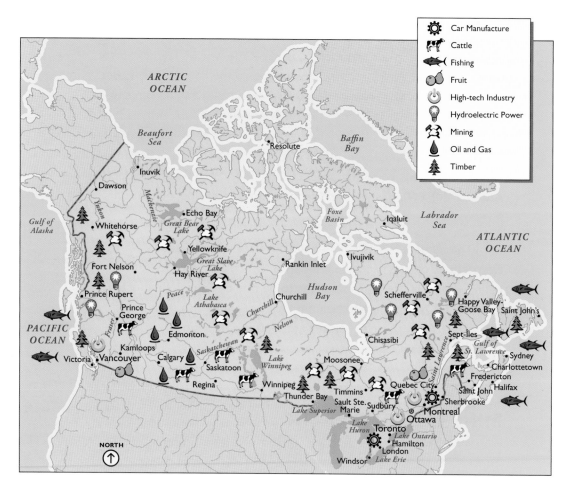

Legend:
- Car Manufacture
- Cattle
- Fishing
- Fruit
- High-tech Industry
- Hydroelectric Power
- Mining
- Oil and Gas
- Timber

ARCTIC OCEAN

Beaufort Sea

Resolute

Baffin Bay

Inuvik

Dawson

Mackenzie

Echo Bay

Great Bear Lake

Foxe Basin

Iqaluit

Labrador Sea

Whitehorse

Yukon

Yellowknife

Great Slave Lake

Rankin Inlet

Ivujivik

ATLANTIC OCEAN

Fort Nelson

Hay River

Prince Rupert

Peace

Lake Athabasca

Churchill

Churchill

Hudson Bay

Schefferville

Happy Valley-Goose Bay

Saint John's

Gulf of Alaska

Prince George

Fraser

Edmonton

Saskatchewan

Nelson

Chisasibi

Sept-Iles

Gulf of St. Lawrence

Sydney

PACIFIC OCEAN

Kamloops

Victoria

Vancouver

Calgary

Saskatoon

Lake Winnipeg

Moosonee

Saint Lawrence

Charlottetown

Fredericton

Halifax

Regina

Winnipeg

Timmins

Thunder Bay

Lake Superior

Sault Ste. Marie

Sudbury

Quebec City

Saint John

Sherbrooke

Montreal

Ottawa

Toronto

Lake Huron

Lake Ontario

Hamilton

London

Windsor

Lake Erie

NORTH
↑

Resources of Canada

cadmium, and titanium. Canada also produces iron ore, gold, copper, silver, lead, and ferroalloys.

Canada ranks third in the world for both mineral and gold production.[8] Diamond production is growing in the Northwest Territories and Nunavut, and the country contributes almost 20 percent of diamonds produced worldwide.[9] Most areas of the country have mineral deposits, which brings the mining industry to areas that may have few other industries. But mining development can cause environmental damage, which is problematic for environmental groups and native groups that own land in the areas being mined.

Canada also has one-sixth of the world's hydroelectric power capacity, supplying much of the country's power needs.[10] New Brunswick and Nova Scotia have large supplies of coal. Canada also has petroleum and natural gas, with the largest fields in Alberta and potential reserves in the Arctic and on the east coast. Pipelines are a necessity for this industry,

HYDROELECTRIC POWER

Canada has a long history of using water to create power. In 1881, the first water wheel was used to produce electricity at the Electric Light Company in Chaudière Falls. Hydroelectric power gradually became the leading source of electricity in Canada. By 2009, approximately 475 hydroelectric-generating plants had sprung up across the country.[11]

and Canada has some of the world's longest natural gas and petroleum pipelines.

MANUFACTURING AND SERVICES

Manufacturing makes up approximately one-fifth of Canada's GDP.[12] The country has a robust steel and iron industry, using the materials to produce motor vehicles, mining equipment, and household appliances. Some other products manufactured and exported from Canada include industrial machinery, aircraft, telecommunications equipment, chemicals, plastics, and fertilizers. Ontario and Quebec are Canada's major manufacturing centers.

The service industry is the largest industry in Canada, employing more than three-fourths of Canadians.[13] One growing service area is tourism. With such natural beauty, Canada is a popular destination for tourists. Tourism supplies more than 600,000 jobs and brings in approximately 2 percent of Canada's GDP. In 2011, that amount was $78.8 billion.[14] A large number of visitors to Canada come from the United States.

INFRASTRUCTURE

Roads make travel easy in the highly populated areas of Canada, but many sparsely populated areas cannot be reached by public roads. In 1962, the

Tourism is a growing segment of Canada's service industry, which employs the majority of Canadians.

Trans-Canada Highway was completed. It spans 4,860 miles (7,821 km) and goes from Saint John's in Newfoundland and Labrador to Victoria in British Columbia.[15] Canada has two transcontinental railway systems: the Canadian National Railway and the Canadian Pacific Railway. Most tracks run east to west in the southern part of the country, but the British Columbia Railway is a major north–south line in the west.

SAINT LAWRENCE SEAWAY

The Saint Lawrence Seaway is a system of locks, canals, and channels that connect the Great Lakes and the Saint Lawrence River with the Atlantic Ocean. It was built in conjunction with the United States and opened to the public in 1959. It allows ships under a certain size to sail from Montreal to Duluth, Minnesota.

Waterways provide vital access to the interiors of Canada and the United States. The Saint Lawrence Seaway, which is 2,342 miles (3,769 km) long, leads toward the head of Lake Superior.[16] This waterway includes the major canals of Canada, such as the Welland Canal and the Sault Sainte Marie Canal.

Airways provide access to otherwise unreachable areas of the country. The main airline is Air Canada, and the largest airport, the Lester B. Pearson International Airport, is located in Toronto. The country

The Canadian Pacific Railway runs though Banff National Park.

CANADA'S CURRENCY

The Canadian dollar was introduced in 1853. Today, the Loonie is the one-dollar coin, named for the loon pictured on it. The Toonie is the two-dollar coin. Other coins come in denominations of 25 cents, ten cents, five cents, and one cent. Canada's copper penny has a picture of a maple leaf on it. Canadian bills come in denominations of five, ten, 20, 50, and 100 dollars. In 2011, the government began phasing paper money out of use. New plastic bills are replacing the paper bills. The bills have raised ink, a see-through window, and numbers hidden in a maple leaf.

also has several smaller airline carriers and charter services. Montreal has two major airports: Pierre Elliot Trudeau and Mirabel.

ECONOMIC CHALLENGES

The biggest problem Canada's economy faces is its dependence on the economic health of the United States, its largest trade partner. This dependence can be beneficial if the US economy is good, but when it is not, Canada feels the full effects. The economies of other world nations can also drag down Canada's economy. The global financial crisis, which began in 2008, caused Canada to enter a recession. But it was able to rebound better than many other countries.

Canadian bills and coins

CHAPTER 9
CANADA TODAY

Modern Canada is a multicultural society with a progressive attitude. French culture and language dominate Quebec and New Brunswick, native cultures dominate the north, and British and immigrant influences are found almost everywhere.

Road signs throughout most of the country are in both French and English. All government documents, Canadian currency, and product packaging are in both languages. Almost 5.2 million people speak both French and English and define themselves as bilingual.[1] Some think bilingualism and multiculturalism create a more open and accepting society.

Canada allows 250,000 immigrants to enter the country each year.

In Toronto's busy Yonge-Dundas Square, Canadians celebrate the achievements of the nation's young people on Youth Day.

117

Canada's Youth in Motion program awards young innovators and leaders under the age of 20 each year. The 2012 winners were:

• Dheevesh Arulmani, age 17, created the Bio-Inspired Photonic Fuel Cell, which uses photosensitizers to enhance electricity production.

• Mingye Chen, age 17, is the president of a local garden club in British Columbia. Her work includes developing a composting program at her school.

• Mirian Dang, age 18, created an educational workshop to educate others about mental health issues.

• Sarah Flaherty, age 16, developed a water filtration system using fabric, a recyclable water bottle, and the sun. Her system was judged by Google to be most likely to positively impact global society.

TEEN LIFE IN CANADA

School is a big part of Canadian teenagers' lives. Education is important to Canadians, and schools have high educational standards. Most children start school with kindergarten, and all must attend first grade. Then they move on to secondary school at age 13 or 14, although some provinces have middle schools in between. All children must attend school from the ages of six to 16. Some families choose to send their children to faith-based public schools. Families also have different kinds of high schools to choose from. Some prepare students for a university education, and others teach trades, such as carpentry, plumbing, or auto repair. The language of instruction is either French or English, but all students must begin learning their nonnative language. In Quebec, students are mostly taught in French. Approximately half of students go on to attend a university or other institution of higher education after high school.[2] This makes for a very literate society—Canada's literacy rate is 99 percent.[3]

Canadian teens listen to music from the United States and watch US television shows in addition to Canadian ones. They also spend a lot of time at malls and movie theaters. Outdoor activities such as camping are popular in the summer months, and skiing and snowboarding are popular in winter. Indoor ice hockey rinks let teens play hockey year-round.

The Internet is an important part of Canadian teens' daily lives. They use it for homework, sending text messages, playing video games, e-mailing, and listening to and downloading music. Social networking is big too. Facebook is the most popular social network. Cyberbullying has become an issue teens face on social networking sites, with one in five teens aged 12 to 17 having witnessed or experienced cyberbullying.[4]

Cold weather doesn't keep Canadian teens indoors. Snowboarding is a favorite winter sport.

CURRENT ISSUES

PRESCRIPTION DRUGS

Many US seniors buy their prescription medications from Canada, where prescription drugs can be much cheaper than in the United States. Some take bus trips to Canada just to buy their medications, and others buy their prescriptions online. It is technically illegal for US citizens to import medications, but the Canadian government allows it as long as each person has proof of a need for the medication and buys only enough for personal use.

An important issue for the Canadian public is improving the country's health care, education, and other social services. In recent years, the federal and provincial governments have reduced funding for these services. A push has been made for social services to be offered through private organizations and institutions rather than through the government.

How to best deliver social services is up for debate. According to the Canadian Medical Association, the country's health-care system is underfunded and has outdated equipment, overcrowded hospitals, and long waiting lists for many nonemergency procedures. Additionally, schools need reforms to better prepare students for useful work after graduation.

Canadians protest the privatization of health care in Ottawa, Ontario.

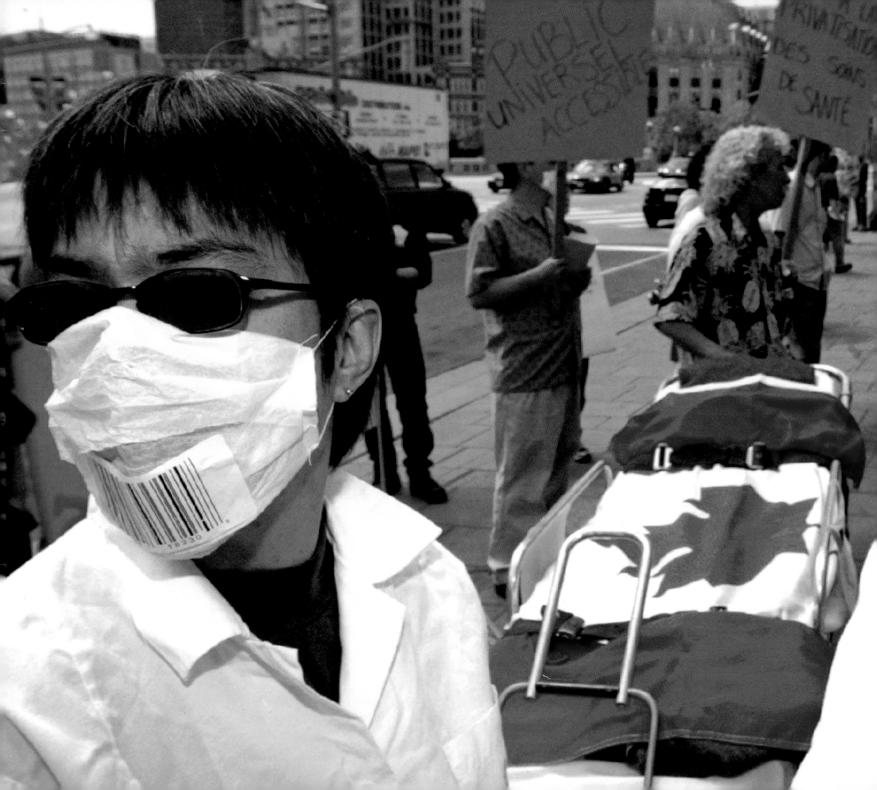

SAME-SEX MARRIAGE IN CANADA

With the passage of the Civil Marriage Act in 2005, same-sex marriage became legal in Canada. The law stated, "Marriage, for civil purposes, is the lawful union of two persons to the exclusion of all others."[6]

Canada's economy continues to grow after the economic downturn, but its health remains linked to that of the US economy. Canada is not as productive as its southern neighbor, partly due to its lack of investment in education, training, and research and development.

Inclusiveness and equality are also important issues, for the French-speaking population as well as the First Nations peoples and immigrants. Many aboriginal peoples have lower standards of living and poorer education systems on their reserves. Aboriginal students have high dropout rates—approximately 51 percent drop out of school before twelfth grade.[5] Additionally, the question of an independent Quebec has not been fully resolved, although it seemed to be less of a priority in 2012.

Drug smuggling is another important issue facing Canada. With such a long US border, people have many opportunities to traffic illegal drugs,

Charles, the Prince of Wales and eldest son of Queen Elizabeth, visits the First Nations University of Canada. The institution is dedicated to meeting the educational needs of First Nations students.

such as marijuana, cocaine, heroin, and ecstasy, between the United States and Canada. Marijuana is the most heavily trafficked drug. Smugglers also transport guns, money, and people. These smugglers sometimes work alone, but most are part of organized crime groups. The United States and Canada are working together to increase border security.

Canada faces ongoing border and boundary disputes. Disputes with the United States are over maritime boundaries at Dixon Entrance, Beaufort Sea, Juan de Fuca Strait, and the Gulf of Maine. Canada is also involved in a sovereignty dispute with Denmark over Hans Island in the Arctic near Greenland.

ECOCONSCIOUS COMMUTING

Cars crowd Canada's urban centers, and pollution is the unfortunate result. Canadian cities are exploring more ecoconscious commuting solutions. These include bike lanes, greenways (long corridors of protected spaces for pedestrian or recreational use), and even wind-powered electric trains. Some ideas that have already been put into practice are car sharing in Toronto and electric vehicle recharging stations in Vancouver.

Canada is also looking to develop its energy resources. These resources could drastically improve Canada's economic growth. But developing these resources can cause severe environmental hazards. Canada aims to find ecologically sound methods of extracting and using its natural energy resources.

Biking instead of driving is one way Canadians go green.

CANADA'S FUTURE

Canada has proven its differences from the United States, but the two countries remain linked in many ways. Trade between them is essential. The two governments will also continue to work together to increase border security. Canada and the United States are each other's most important allies. Prime Minister Stephen Harper has said the United States "is and always will be our closest neighbor, our greatest ally, and our best friend."[7]

As new immigrants enter the country, Canada's multicultural identity is constantly being redefined. To support its increasing population, Canada must also develop ways to increase its productivity. Energy may be the key to Canada's continued success. With its abundance of natural resources, Canada's future looks bright. Its diverse peoples will continue to thrive for years to come.

National pride helps diverse Canadians find a common identity.

[TIMELINE]

12,000 years ago	Humans leave evidence of habitation on Haida Gwaii.
1008	Viking Thorfinn Karlsefni and his group settle in Newfoundland at the site of L'Anse aux Meadows.
1497	On June 24, John Cabot arrives in Canada and claims the land for England.
1534	Jacques Cartier arrives and claims land along the Saint Lawrence River for France.
1608	French explorer Samuel de Champlain arrives and builds a settlement, which is the beginning of New France.
1610	Hudson Bay is discovered by English explorer Henry Hudson.
1670	The Hudson's Bay Company is established, gaining a monopoly on the Canadian fur trade.
1759	The Battle of Abraham Plains, a battle in the Seven Years' War, takes place on September 13.
1760	Horses are introduced to Sable Island, where their descendants roam in wild herds today.
1763	The Treaty of Paris is signed, ending the Seven Years' War and giving the British the rights to New France.
1764	The Niagara Treaty is signed, promising peaceful relations between the First Nations bands and the British.
1774	The Quebec Act is signed, giving religious and legal rights to the French in the province.

1812	The United States declares war and invades Canada in June.
1814	The Treaty of Ghent is signed, ending the War of 1812 and settling the eastern border between the United States and Canada.
1867	On July 1, the British North America Act is signed, uniting the colonies and forming the Dominion of Canada.
1870	The new province of Manitoba is added as a land for the Métis people.
1913	Immigration to Canada peaks.
1914	World War I begins and Canadian troops show their support for Britain, gaining international recognition for their efforts.
1931	The Statute of Westminster is passed, granting Canada autonomy from Britain.
1949	The islands of Haida Gwaii are hit with Canada's strongest recorded earthquake.
1980	A referendum for the sovereignty of Quebec is put to the vote but does not pass.
1982	The Charter of Rights and Freedoms is added to the Canadian Constitution.
1999	The territory of Nunavut is established in the Inuit homeland on April 1.
2006	On February 6, Stephen Harper is sworn in as the prime minister. He remains in power as of 2012.

FACTS AT YOUR FINGERTIPS

GEOGRAPHY

Official name: Canada

Area: 3,855,103 square miles (9,984,670 sq km)

Climate: Varies from temperate in south to subarctic and Arctic in north.

Highest elevation: Mount Logan, 19,550 feet (5,959 m) above sea level

Lowest elevation: Atlantic Ocean, 0 feet (0 m) below sea level

Significant geographic features: Canada is the world's largest country that borders only one country. It also boasts the Canadian Shield, Rocky Mountains, Coast Mountains, Great Lakes, and Mackenzie River.

PEOPLE

Population (July 2012 est.): 34,300,083

Most populous city: Toronto

Ethnic groups: British Isles origin, 28 percent; French origin, 23 percent; other European, 15 percent; Amerindian, 2 percent; other (mostly Asian, African, or Arab), 6 percent; mixed background, 26 percent

Percentage of residents living in urban areas: 81 percent

Life expectancy: 81.48 years at birth (world rank: 12)

Languages: English, French

Religions: Roman Catholic, 42.6 percent; Protestant, 23.3 percent (United Church, 9.5 percent; Anglican, 6.8 percent; Baptist, 2.4 percent; Lutheran,

2 percent); other Christian,
4.4 percent; Muslim, 1.9 percent;
other and unspecified, 11.8 percent;
none, 16 percent

GOVERNMENT AND ECONOMY

Government: a parliamentary
democracy, a federation, and a
constitutional monarchy

Capital: Ottawa

Date of adoption of current
constitution: March 29, 1867, and
April 17, 1982

Head of state: monarch represented
in Canada by a governor-general

Head of government: prime
minister

Legislature: bicameral Parliament,
consists of the Senate and the
House of Commons

Currency: Canadian dollar

Industries and natural resources:
Industries include transportation
equipment, chemicals, processed

and unprocessed minerals, food
products, wood and paper products,
fish products, petroleum, and
natural gas. Natural resources
include iron ore, nickel, zinc,
copper, gold, lead, rare earth
elements, molybdenum, potash,
diamonds, silver, fish, timber, wildlife,
coal, petroleum, natural gas, and
hydropower.

NATIONAL SYMBOLS

Holidays: Canada Day on July 1 celebrates the formation of the Dominion of Canada.

Flag: Two vertical bands of red with a white square between them; an 11-pointed red maple leaf is centered in the white square. The maple leaf has long been a Canadian symbol, and the official colors of Canada are red and white.

National anthem: "O Canada"

National animal: beaver

KEY PEOPLE

John Cabot, first British explorer, claimed Newfoundland for England

Samuel de Champlain, claimed Quebec area for France

PROVINCES AND TERRITORIES OF CANADA

Province or Territory; Capital

Alberta; Edmonton

British Columbia; Victoria

Manitoba; Winnipeg

New Brunswick; Fredericton

Newfoundland and Labrador; Saint John's

Northwest Territories; Yellowknife

Nova Scotia; Halifax

Nunavut; Iqaluit

Ontario; Toronto

Prince Edward Island; Charlottetown

Quebec; Quebec City

Saskatchewan; Regina

Yukon; Whitehorse

GLOSSARY

advocate

To publicly recommend or support.

affluent

Having a great deal of money or wealth.

autonomy

The right or condition of self-government.

biome

A large, natural community of animals and plants occupying a major habitat.

boreal

Of or relating to the north.

coniferous

Trees that bear cones and evergreen needles or scalelike leaves.

deciduous

A type of plant or tree that sheds its leaves annually.

fortified

Strengthened so it is protected against attack.

funicular

A mountainside railroad operating by cable with descending and ascending cars.

hypothermia

The condition of having an abnormally low body temperature.

integral

   Necessary to make a whole complete.

Métis

   Mixed-race people of combined indigenous and European ancestry.

pastoral

   Associated with country life.

permafrost

   A thick layer of soil below the surface that remains frozen throughout the year.

philanthropic

   Seeking to promote the welfare of others.

referendum

   A vote by an entire electorate on a specific question or questions.

sovereignty

   Supreme power or authority.

sporadically

   Occurring at irregular intervals.

ADDITIONAL RESOURCES

SELECTED BIBLIOGRAPHY

Brokaw, Leslie, et al. *Frommer's Canada.* Mississauga, ON: Wiley, 2011. Print.

Brown, Craig, ed. *The Illustrated History of Canada.* Toronto: Key Porter, 2007. Print.

Canadian Encyclopedia. Canadian Encyclopedia, 2012. Web. 27 Sept. 2012.

Harris, Georgina, Michelle de Larrabeiti, and Zoe Ross, eds. *Canada.* New York: DK, 2012. Print.

Thompson, Wayne C. *Canada.* Lanham, MD: Stryker-Post, 2012. Print.

Zimmerman, Karla, et al. *Discover Canada.* Footscray, AU: Lonely Planet, 2011. Print.

FURTHER READINGS

Laws, Gordon D., and Lauren M. Laws. *Manitoba.* San Diego: Lucent, 2003. Print.

Laws, Gordon D., and Lauren M. Laws. *The Maritime Provinces.* San Diego: Lucent, 2004. Print.

Mayell, Mark. *Newfoundland.* San Diego: Lucent, 2003. Print.

WEB LINKS

To learn more about Canada, visit ABDO Publishing Company online at **www.abdopublishing.com**. Web sites about Canada are featured on our Book Links page. These links are routinely monitored and updated to provide the most current information available.

PLACES TO VISIT

If you are ever in Canada, consider checking out these important and interesting sites!

Banff National Park
Located in the Rocky Mountains of Alberta, this stunning park has snow-tipped peaks, wildflower meadows, and the beautiful Lake Louise.

The Canadian Museum of Civilization
This architecturally stunning museum in Quebec has exhibits about the different peoples and history of Canada.

Haida Heritage Site, Haida Gwaii
See unique species of animals and plants on this archipelago, and visit the remains of a Haida village with amazing examples of totem poles.

L'Anse aux Meadows National Historic Site
Found at the tip of Newfoundland, this is the site of the Viking settlement and has three reconstructions of Norse buildings.

Niagara Falls
See the powerful Horseshoe Falls in southern Ontario.

[SOURCE NOTES]

CHAPTER 1. A VISIT TO CANADA

1. "Fortifications of Quebec National Historic Site." *Parks Canada.* Parks Canada, 18 Jan. 2012. Web. 27 Sept. 2012.

2. Annie Graves. "Weekend: Quebec City." *Yankee.* Yankee, 2010. Web. 27 Sept. 2012.

3. "The World Factbook: Canada." *Central Intelligence Agency.* Central Intelligence Agency, 11 Sept. 2012. Web. 27 Sept. 2012.

CHAPTER 2. GEOGRAPHY: AN ANCIENT AND WILD LAND

1. "Canadian Shield." *Encyclopædia Britannica.* Encyclopædia Britannica, 2012. Web. 6 Sept. 2012.

2. Ibid.

3. "The World Factbook: Canada." *Central Intelligence Agency.* Central Intelligence Agency, 11 Sept. 2012. Web. 27 Sept. 2012.

4. "Physiographic Regions." *Canadian Encyclopedia.* Canadian Encyclopedia, 2012. Web. 27 Sept. 2012.

5. "Canadian Landforms." *Canadian Geographic.* Canadian Geographic, n.d. Web. 27 Sept. 2012.

6. "Mackenzie River." *Encyclopædia Britannica.* Encyclopædia Britannica, 2012. Web. 6 Sept. 2012.

7. "The World Factbook: Canada." *Central Intelligence Agency.* Central Intelligence Agency, 11 Sept. 2012. Web. 27 Sept. 2012.

8. "Physiographic Regions." *Canadian Encyclopedia.* Canadian Encyclopedia, 2012. Web. 27 Sept. 2012.

9. "Canada." *Weatherbase.* Canty and Associates, n.d. Web. 27 Sept. 2012.

10. "Point Pelee National Park of Canada, Ontario." *Southern Ontario Tourism.* Southern Ontario Tourism Organization, 2006. Web. 27 Sept. 2012.

11. Georgina Harris, Michelle de Larrabeiti, and Zoe Ross, eds. *Canada.* New York: DK, 2012. Print. 213.

12. "Atlantic Region." *Canadian Geographic.* Canadian Geographic, n.d. Web. 27 Sept. 2012.

13. "Atlantic Maritime Ecozone." *Ecological Framework of Canada.* Ecological Framework of Canada, n.d. Web. 27 Sept. 2012.

14. Ibid.

CHAPTER 3. ANIMALS AND NATURE: ABUNDANT LIFE IN CANADA'S BIOMES

1. "The Atlas of Canada: Boreal Forest." *Natural Resources Canada.* Natural Resources Canada, 27 Apr. 2009. Web. 27 Sept. 2012.

2. "Parks Canada and Plains Bison." *Parks Canada.* Parks Canada, 22 Aug. 2012. Web. 27 Sept. 2012.

3. "Sable Island, Known for Its Wild Horses, Is Now a National Park." *HorseChannel.com.* BowTie, 2012. Web. 27 Sept. 2012.

4. "Canada's 44 National Parks." *CBC News.* CBC, 22 Aug. 2012. Web. 27 Sept. 2012.

5. "Overview of Climate Change in Canada." *Natural Resources Canada.* Natural Resources Canada, 22 Oct. 2009. Web. 27 Sept. 2012.

6. "Summary Statistics: Summaries by Country, Table 5, Threatened Species in Each Country." *IUCN Red List of Threatened Species*. International Union for Conservation of Nature and Natural Resources, 2011. Web. 27 Sept. 2012.

CHAPTER 4. HISTORY: FROM FRONTIER TO INDEPENDENCE

1. "The Viking Saga to 1400." *History of Canada Online*. History of Canada Online, 1 Mar. 2012. Web. 27 Sept. 2012.

2. Georgina Harris, Michelle de Larrabeiti, and Zoe Ross, eds. *Canada*. New York: DK, 2012. Print. 62.

3. "Growth & Change in B. N. A." *History of Canada Online*. History of Canada Online, 15 Mar. 2012. Web. 27 Sept. 2012.

4. "Klondike Gold Rush." *Encyclopædia Britannica*. Encyclopædia Britannica, 2012. Web. 27 Sept. 2012.

5. "A Time of Transition: Canada after 1945." *History of Canada Online*. History of Canada Online, 2 Dec. 2011. Web. 27 Sept. 2012.

6. Diana Breti. "Internment Camps in British Columbia." *VancouverIsland.com*. Simon Fraser University, 1998. Web. 27 Sept. 2012.

CHAPTER 5. PEOPLE: A CULTURAL MOSAIC

1. Right Honorable Pierre Elliott Trudeau. "Pierre Elliott Trudeau Multiculturalism." *Canada History*. Canada History, 2012. Web. 27 Sept. 2012.

2. "The Atlas of Canada: Languages." *Natural Resources Canada*. Natural Resources Canada, 13 Nov. 2009. Web. 27 Sept. 2012.

3. "The World Factbook: Canada." *Central Intelligence Agency*. Central Intelligence Agency, 11 Sept. 2012. Web. 27 Sept. 2012.

4. "The Atlas of Canada: Population Density." *Natural Resources Canada*. Natural Resources Canada, 4 Nov. 2009. Web. 27 Sept. 2012.

5. "Ethnic Identity." *Canadian Encyclopedia*. Canadian Encyclopedia, 2012. Web. 27 Sept. 2012.

6. "The World Factbook: Canada." *Central Intelligence Agency*. Central Intelligence Agency, 11 Sept. 2012. Web. 27 Sept. 2012.

7. Ibid.

8. "British Home Child: Historical Overview." *Citizenship and Immigration Canada*. Citizenship and Immigration Canada, 22 July 2010. Web. 27 Sept. 2012.

9. "The World Factbook: Canada." *Central Intelligence Agency*. Central Intelligence Agency, 11 Sept. 2012. Web. 27 Sept. 2012.

10. "Aboriginal Peoples." *Statistics Canada*. Statistics Canada, 12 Nov. 2009. Web. 27 Sept. 2012.

11. "Canada." *Encyclopædia Britannica*. Encyclopædia Britannica, 2012. Web. 27 Sept. 2012.

12. "2006 Census." *Statistics Canada*. Statistics Canada, 22 Sept. 2009. Web. 27 Sept. 2012.

13. "Canada." *Encyclopædia Britannica*. Encyclopædia Britannica, 2012. Web. 27 Sept. 2012.

SOURCE NOTES CONTINUED

14. "The World Factbook: Canada." *Central Intelligence Agency.* Central Intelligence Agency, 11 Sept. 2012. Web. 27 Sept. 2012.

15. "The Chinese Community in Canada." *Statistics Canada.* Statistics Canada, 15 Mar. 2005. Web. 27 Sept. 2012.

16. "The World Factbook: Canada." *Central Intelligence Agency.* Central Intelligence Agency, 11 Sept. 2012. Web. 27 Sept. 2012.

17. Ibid.

18. Ibid.

19. Ibid.

20. "The Atlas of Canada: Religious Affiliation." *Natural Resources Canada.* Natural Resources Canada, 12 Sept. 2009. Web. 27 Sept. 2012.

21. "The World Factbook: Canada." *Central Intelligence Agency.* Central Intelligence Agency, 11 Sept. 2012. Web. 27 Sept. 2012.

22. Terry Watada. "Buddhism in Canada." *Jodo Shinsu Buddhist Temples of Canada.* Jodo Shinsu Buddhist Temples of Canada, 2010. Web. 27 Sept. 2012.

23. "Mennonites." *Canadian Encyclopedia.* Canadian Encyclopedia, 2012. Web. 27 Sept. 2012.

CHAPTER 6. CULTURE: IN CONSTANT EVOLUTION

1. Steve Keating. "Hockey Is More Than a Game to Canadians." *Reuters.* Thomson Reuters, 29 Jan. 2010. Web. 26 Jun. 2012.

2. "Teams." *NHL.* NHL, 2012. Web. 27 Sept. 2012.

3. "Skyscrapers." *Canadian Encyclopedia.* Canadian Encyclopedia, 2012. Web. 27 Sept. 2012.

4. Wayne C. Thompson. *Canada.* Lanham, MD: Stryker-Post, 2012. Print. 6.

CHAPTER 7. POLITICS: BRITISH BASIS AND CANADIAN GOALS

1. "Constitution Act, 1982. Part I." *Department of Justice Canada.* Department of Justice Canada, 27 Sept. 2012. Web. 27 Sept. 2012.

CHAPTER 8. ECONOMICS: AN AFFLUENT COUNTRY

1. "The World Factbook: Canada." *Central Intelligence Agency.* Central Intelligence Agency, 11 Sept. 2012. Web. 27 Sept. 2012.

2. "International Human Development Indicators: Canada." *United Nations Development Programme.* United Nations Development Programme, 2011. Web. 27 Sept. 2012.

3. "The World Factbook: Canada." *Central Intelligence Agency.* Central Intelligence Agency, 11 Sept. 2012. Web. 27 Sept. 2012.

4. "Canada." *Encyclopædia Britannica.* Encyclopædia Britannica, 2012. Web. 27 Sept. 2012.

5. "The World Factbook: Canada." *Central Intelligence Agency.* Central Intelligence Agency, 11 Sept. 2012. Web. 27 Sept. 2012.

6. "Canada." *Encyclopædia Britannica*. Encyclopædia Britannica, 2012. Web. 27 Sept. 2012.

7. Wayne C. Thompson. *Canada*. Lanham, MD: Stryker-Post, 2012. Print. 180.

8. Ibid. 182.

9. Levon Sevunts. "Canada: Diamond Mining Superpower." *Alaska Dispatch*. Alaska Dispatch, 1 Sept. 2012. Web. 27 Sept. 2012.

10. "Canada." *Encyclopædia Britannica*. Encyclopædia Britannica, 2012. Web. 27 Sept. 2012.

11. Canadian Hydropower Association. "Hydropower in Canada: Past, Present, and Future." *RenewableEnergyWorld.com*. RenewableEnergyWorld.com, 1 Oct. 2009. Web. 27 Sept. 2012.

12. "Canada." *Encyclopædia Britannica*. Encyclopædia Britannica, 2012. Web. 27 Sept. 2012.

13. "The World Factbook: Canada." *Central Intelligence Agency*. Central Intelligence Agency, 11 Sept. 2012. Web. 27 Sept. 2012.

14. "Industry Overview." *Supporting Tourism*. Government of Canada, 13 Aug. 2012. Web. 27 Sept. 2012.

15. "Canada." *Encyclopædia Britannica*. Encyclopædia Britannica, 2012. Web. 27 Sept. 2012.

16. Ibid.

CHAPTER 9. CANADA TODAY

1. Benoit Hardy-Vallée. "Canadian Bilingualism: Pourquoi C'est Important." *Canadian Newcomer*. Canadian Newcomer Magazine, 2012. Web. 27 Sept. 2012.

2. "Education at a Glance 2012: OECD Report Finds U.S. Lags Behind Other Countries in Higher Education Attainment Rate." *Huffington Post*. Huffington Post, 11 Sept. 2012. Web. 27 Sept. 2012.

3. "The World Factbook: Canada." *Central Intelligence Agency*. Central Intelligence Agency, 11 Sept. 2012. Web. 27 Sept. 2012.

4. "The Internet a New School Yard for Bullies?" *Ipsos*. Ipsos North America, 20 Mar. 2012. Web. 27 Sept. 2012.

5. Robert Laboucane. "Canada's Aboriginal Education Crisis." *AMMSA*. Aboriginal Multi-Media Society, 2010. Web. 27 Sept. 2012.

6. "Civil Marriage Act." *Department of Justice Canada*. Department of Justice Canada, 2005. Web. 27 Sept. 2012.

7. Paul Koring. "Looser Border Restrictions a Top Priority, Obama Signals to Harper." *Globe and Mail*. Globe and Mail, 6 Sept. 2012. Web. 27 Sept. 2012.

[INDEX]

PHOTO CREDITS